What people are saying about…

STORIES UNLEASHED

"A rare but deep—and immensely inspiring—look into what makes people successful! A constant theme you'll find throughout is beginning with a deep desire, a willingness to learn the right strategies, a bias toward action, and the ability to bounce back again and again and again. Add to that a potent belief in one's mission and, ultimately, a powerful belief in themselves, and the end result becomes undeniable. This is a book for anyone committed to living a life both professionally fulfilling and personally joyful."

—Bob Burg
Coauthor of, "The Go-Giver"

"Whether you're an entrepreneur, a leader, or anyone looking for a path forward, Genius Unleashed is packed with insights you won't find elsewhere. Christie's story of perseverance is not only motivating but provides concrete lessons that will guide others through life's challenges. A must-read for anyone who wants to transform their story!"

—Tom Matzen
Serial Entrepreneur

"A call to freedom! Casey McDonald's longing for more and her bold actions are an inspiration to many of us who, like her, have a soul on fire moment as we're trapped in a life we're unhappy with."

—Mark Whiskey
Entrepreneur

"Kathy Mayeda shares deeply how learning to trust and follow her inner guidance is something we can all take to heart. It shows that support is all around us, although most of the time it seems invisible. I love how Kathy learns to not only see this guidance but to trust that there is something there in spite of challenges. These challenges are not meant to stop us but to also guide us along our path. Big takeaway from reading this, stay true to your path and know it's unique for you! What a gift!"

—Aimee Brimhall McCord
Founder of Inspirational Horse

"Casey McDonald's story offers a concept to ponder: what else is out there generating wealth, knowledge application, and true legacy beyond the norm we're taught? The author's reach into her own life experience and challenge shows that one can shift the track others set forth for us. Though the story is short, it offers a perspective that shifts the status quo into creation with Casey as the guide."

—EM Finley

"Kathy Mayeda's story is a testament to the resilience of the human spirit and the profound wisdom available when we listen to our bodies and the natural world. From corporate layoffs to physical injury, from devastating loss to visibility fears, Kathy's journey reveals how our deepest wounds become our greatest teachers. Her chapter beautifully illustrates what becomes possible when we trust our intuition to guide us back to our innate healing capacity. This is an essential read for anyone navigating transition, loss, or the courageous path from hiding to healing, and a powerful reminder that we can always find our way back to ourselves."

—Sara Powers
Intuitive Business Coach and Consulting Astrologer

"Dr. Neja throws light on how we tend to compartmentalise life and how being truly successful requires the integration and alignment of its mental, emotional, somatic, and spiritual aspects. They are not separate, requiring specialist input for healing in each; rather, they are integrated, and once aligned, every part of life—health, finances, business, and relationships—takes off.

Neja's personal story is a powerful, beautifully poignant vehicle for bringing her work to life."

—Wendy Corner
CEO, Speaker, Speaker Coach, Author, Podcaster, TEDx Trainer

"Genius Unleashed is filled with transformational stories, and Jannette's chapter is one of the true gems. Her voice is authentic, insightful, and deeply encouraging, offering readers a beautiful blend of inspiration and practical wisdom."

—Dr Barry Auchettl
Life Visionary

"Kathy Mayeda's story in Genius Unleashed is a powerful testament to resilience and transformation. I love how she blended and braided her experiences as a horsewoman, designer, and healer, especially for anyone who has felt lost in the pursuit of purpose or recovery from injury and loss."

—Heather LeFevre
Craniosacral Therapist, Author

"Jannette Anderson's chapter grabbed me by the heart from the first line and didn't let go. Jannette shows, with unshakeable honesty, how reinvention is possible at any age, and why your next chapter can be your best chapter. A must-read for anyone ready to rise."

—Quynh Vo
Founder of www.AIstartupCEO.com

"Dr. Neja Zupan's story is an inspiring and powerful read! The book provides real stories of grit and resilience, paired with practical strategies to help readers overcome obstacles and achieve their dreams.

This is more than just a book; it's a toolkit for anyone ready to step into their potential."

—Murari Garodia
International Business Entrepreneur

"I absolutely love stories that give me glimpses into the author's imperfect journey. Success rarely arrives riding in a limousine. Instead, it's usually found by trudging up crumbling steps, one at a time. Mastery Unleashed is filled with such stories–including one from a coach, entrepreneur, and thought leader that I truly respect and admire, Christie Ruffino. Her story is inspiring, and her ability to help entrepreneurs and coaches is truly a gift. She's a real-life hero to me."

—Jeff C. West
Award-Winning Coauthor of, "Streetwise to Saleswise"

"An inspiring and powerful read! The book provides real stories of grit and resilience, paired with practical strategies to help readers overcome obstacles and achieve their dreams.

This is more than just a book; it's a toolkit for anyone ready to step into their potential."

—Murari Garodia
International Business Entrepreneur

"Mastery Unleashed is filled with transformational stories, and Jannette's chapter is one of the true gems. Her voice is authentic, insightful, and deeply encouraging, offering readers a beautiful blend of inspiration and practical wisdom."

—Dr Barry Auchettl
Life Visionary

"What a wonderful inspiration and powerful collection of stories representing triumphs, challenges, and success. This book comes with the same inspiration and enthusiasm that Christie shows in her workshops and coaching. She makes you feel like you can do whatever you put your mind to, and with just enough of a shove, you find yourself in it. Seeing what others have done and how they came into their success is always inspirational to me. Mastery Unleashed is for everyone, no matter if you're just starting out or looking for inspiration on your personal journey, you'll find it here. Thank you, Christie (again)!!"

—Frederick L. McQueen

"Mastery Unleashed is an exceptional collection of stories that beautifully balances vulnerability and strength—a truly winning combination. Each contributor shares their personal journey with honesty and courage, offering inspiring lessons and powerful insights. The authenticity in every story makes this anthology deeply relatable and motivating. Christie Ruffino has, once again, curated a book that not only empowers readers but also reminds us of the resilience within all of us. Highly recommend for anyone seeking inspiration and real-life examples of perseverance and growth."

—Self Help Guru

"Mastery Unleashed is an inspiring collection of stories from individuals who have achieved remarkable success in business, health, and personal development. This anthology doesn't just showcase their accomplishments; it dives into the real, behind-the-scenes moments that shaped their journeys. The honesty and relatability of each story make it impossible to put down.

What sets this book apart is its practicality. Each contributor goes beyond sharing their experiences by offering actionable tools and strategies that readers can immediately apply. Whether you're aiming to advance in your career, improve your well-being, or embark on a journey of personal growth, the lessons within these pages provide a clear path forward."

—Connor Hiebel

"Mastery Unleashed: Stories & Strategies to Unleash Potential is more than just a book—it's an inspiring roadmap for anyone ready to break through barriers and reach their highest potential. Through a masterful blend of compelling stories and actionable strategies, the book captures the essence of what it means to grow, transform, and thrive in both life and work.

The stories are relatable and deeply human, offering glimpses into the lives of individuals who've faced challenges similar to our own. Whether it's overcoming fear, finding confidence, or stepping into uncharted territory, the narratives remind us that transformation is not only possible but well within our grasp."

—K. J. Stultz
Certified Integrative Wellness Coach and Healer

"This is an excellent read of wisdom, grace, courage, and excitement. The stories of navigating life experiences and making choices bring to light all the possibilities one faces. Showing the human side and the spiritual side of life's smorgasbord of the realities we create."

—Dr. Susan Taffer

"Traveling through the journeys of the authors in Christie Ruffino's Mastery Unleashed is nothing short of inspiring. Their stories evoke awe, emotion, and admiration as they navigate waves of despair and darkness, yet emerge with unwavering grit, determination, faith, and passion. Their ability to transform hardship into unimaginable success is truly commendable.

By sharing their experiences and offering valuable insights into the path to success, these authors provide readers with a generous gift. Christie Ruffino's vision in bringing them together has resulted in a remarkable and praiseworthy anthology."

—Minoti Rajput,
Author, Speaker, and Entrepreneur

What our clients are saying about…

UNLEASHED PUBLISHING

"Christie turned my life story into something so powerful it brought me to tears. I felt seen, understood, and inspired by my own journey. She made the process incredibly easy and captured the depth of my experience better than I ever could on my own."

—Marina Tudor
Licensed Psychotherapist

"Working with Christie was an opportunity not to be missed. She explained every step so clearly, and the entire process felt simple and well-thought-out. The step-by-step guidance made authoring the book feel doable, and having the marketing handled took so much stress off. The support, hand-holding, and help with the writing were always there when needed. This process truly delivers what it promises, and I'm grateful to have been part of it."

— Alexia Clonda
Breathing and Mindset Coach

"I really loved the ChatGPT-powered first draft Christie gave me. It was an excellent foundation and helped me create an even better version of my story."

— Dr. Neja Zupan
Global Energy Master

"I had been working on launching a program for a long time, and within a couple of months of working with Christie, my program was launched, with clients paying thousands of dollars to be part of it."

—Tracy Eisenman
High-Performance Coach

"So much VALUE from your program! Thank you for going on this journey with me. In just ONE WEEK, I have received so much VALUE from your program. Wow. I'm not sure I would have ever arrived at this process/strategy for high-ticket pricing. I would still be lost and wasting time on endless iterations."

—Melissa Unsell-Smith
CEO, Catalytic Icon

"Christie Ruffino has catapulted storytelling to Oscar status as she empowers future authors to create their best work with her hands-on, fun, interactive workshop powered by AI. Walking you through each step to optimize results, the creation process is nothing short of genius, igniting your unique story into an epic tale that captivates, compels, and connects with your ideal audience. It's the most exciting and brilliant story-writing course you'll ever take!"

—Jane Applegath
Founder Epic Vision Zone

"Being an author in the latest book in the 'Overcoming Mediocrity' series helped me break through a limiting block so I can share my story. Christie helped me gain confidence and realize that by sharing my story, I'm helping others and positioning myself as a subject matter expert. Now, I'm getting invited to be on other people's podcasts. I'm considering starting my own podcast as well. If you have an important story inside you, Christie and the company she founded has resources to help you share it in a big and impactful way."

—Therese R. Nicklas, CFP®, CMC®
Certified Financial Planner™ and True Wealth™ Coach

"I hit six figures in my first year, and I'm doing really well, thanks to Christie's coaching and the publicity that I was able to get from the overcoming mediocrity series. I can't recommend this experience highly enough. Joining the overcoming mediocrity team was a life-changing experience for me."

—Lindsey Oaks
Personal Branding

"If you're on the fence, I'd highly recommend and encourage you to jump in feet first because not only did I get to work with other amazing women, but I also ended up being an Amazon Bestselling Author which is a huge boost for my career and brand. I hope that you'll choose to share your inspiring story for all of the many women who are going to read it."

—Amber Champagne-Matos
Founder of Champagne Apothecary

"More freedom serving more clients! Since I'm on a mission to help people recharge their digestive systems so they can feel and live better, I love that my new group program business model allows me to spend my time more wisely and help more people."

— Dr. Marilu Hunt, Pharm.D.
Integrative Nutrition Health Coach and Gut Health Specialist

"I cannot say enough about Christie Ruffino and her coaching! I found so much value that I chose to collaborate with her on the most recent publication of Overcoming Mediocrity. You will not be disappointed when you reach out to Christie for coaching in business, as the insight, tools, and coaching elements also translate to everyday life."

—Sara Goggin Young
Owner, Mindset, Nutrition, and Movement Coach

"Working with Christie and her team was just the nudge I needed to finally sit down and start writing. The social media tips that were provided when the book launched were invaluable for engaging and re-engaging people who follow me. I am much more confident about my next book, and its launch."

—Valerie Mrak
Speaker • Filmmaker • Storyteller • Coach

"I'm passionate about helping women overcome the lies that are holding them back. The problem was that I still believed my own lies. I questioned if my story could actually make a difference, feared that no one would want to hear it and didn't trust I could write it well enough for it to be published. Until I met Christie. She invited me to share my story in one of her books, and it completely transformed my business, my life, and best of all, the lives of the women who read it. They've reached out to me, grateful for how what I shared helped them overcome their adversities. Hearing those women's testimonies gave me confidence and fueled me to keep writing. With Christie's help, I published my own book just a few months later, and am currently writing the next in that series."

—Shannon Ferraby
Author, Speaker, and Trainer with Success Unwrapped

"Being a part of this book made such a difference and I love the conversations that Christie and I had together. They were so rich and revealing that I actually can do a TED talk. But really, what really broke through for me is being able to share my story and to be a subject expert. Since then, I've been on other people's podcasts and I started my own podcast 'Tea Time Midlife Edition.' If you have a story that you want to share with the world, get in front of Christie."

—Regina Young
Podcaster and CEO of Modelperfect Woman

"Being an author in the series has opened doors for me. It makes it easier to rise to the top of the list for those responsible for booking speaking gigs to want to talk to me. The traffic to my website and Business Page has increased measurably. It has shortened the know, like, trust factor. People are reaching out to me first before I reach out to them. The titles of the books help women who want to stretch themselves. Who wouldn't want to associate themselves and work with an author who is Dynamic, Resilient, Strong, and Influential?"

—Jeanne Lyons
Career Breakthrough Coach

"Being an Amazon Bestselling Author alongside some fabulous women in this series has propelled me forward in ways that I wouldn't have had otherwise. I've since guested on podcasts, I have an episode on Amazon Fire TV, and I've had so many women tell me how inspired they've been by the book. Secondarily, I was able to tell my story in a really authentic way and not have it completely rearranged in the editing process. I'm really excited to see what the future holds."

—Tiffany Lewis
CEO of More Meaningful Marketing

"Christie is a mission-driven woman who is changing the world by sharing the stories of amazing women. I was honored to be included in one of her bestselling books, and the benefits of that book keep unfolding in my life. The impact in my life started immediately with writing my story (an impactful internal journey to my own personal why), continued with the connections I made to the other women in the book AND in Christie's extensive network, and continues because I'm now a best-selling author, speaker, and podcaster. It really launched a whole new chapter in my life. If you are ready to embrace the next iteration of yourself and make a difference in the world, contact Christie."

—Maren Oslac
Founder of Heart & Sole Dance

"Christie Ruffino is a master at taking women's women who are passionate about telling their story, but they don't know exactly how they're going to do it and molding us into not only authors but Amazon Bestselling Authors. It was an amazing six-month journey, where I got to meet some amazing women, discover their stories, and realize that what I have to say is important and something that the world needs to hear."

—Danica Joan
Founder of Kids Need Both, Inc.

"Christie and her team made the process of becoming an Amazon Bestselling Author easy and fun. There are resources and support every step of the way, and now I have a book to grow my business."

—Amanda Tobinski
Magnetic Media Group

"Christie and the OM team took an overwhelming and complicated process of book publishing and made it very easy to get my story published. I was guided through the process from start to finish. Every detail was outlined, and my questions were always answered promptly. The book has received rave reviews, and it has taken my credibility to the next level, as I am now an Amazon #1 best seller! Thank you!!"

—Lynn O'Dowd
Motivational Speaker and Keynote Performer

"Me, an Amazon number one Bestselling Author. What a crazy exciting journey this has been and an accomplishment I would have never dreamed of. Joining the Overcoming Mediocrity project has brought me so many new connections, as well as the credibility and the credentials for my business. Becoming an author is something I never planned to do in my lifetime but has been a very, very exciting ride!"

—Laura Fank-Carrara
President of Laura Ocean Solutions

GENIUS UNLEASHED

Other Books By Christie

Seven Figure Book Launch

Mastery Unleashed

Treasured Tribes

Story to Authority

One Simple Phrase

Dare to Be a Difference Maker Volume 2

Overcoming Mediocrity Series

Overcoming Mediocrity — Dynamic Women

Overcoming Mediocrity — Courageous Women

Overcoming Mediocrity — Strong Women

Overcoming Mediocrity — Remarkable Women

Overcoming Mediocrity — Resilient Women

Overcoming Mediocrity — Influential Women

Overcoming Mediocrity — Victorious Women

Overcoming Mediocrity — Fearless Women

Overcoming Mediocrity — Unstoppable Women

Overcoming Mediocrity — Empowered Women

Overcoming Mediocrity — Limitless Women

Overcoming Mediocrity — Epic Women

Stories and Strategies to Unlock Your Brilliance

GENIUS UNLEASHED

Genius Unleashed is a powerful collection of real-world stories from entrepreneurs who turned struggle into strength and setbacks into momentum. Filled with practical wisdom, hard-won insights, and proven strategies, this book will challenge you to think bigger, build resilience, and move forward with courage—no matter the obstacles.

Presented by Christie Ruffino

Unleashed Publishing

www.MasteryUnleashedCoaching.com

This book is a compilation of stories from numerous experts who have each contributed a chapter. It is designed to provide information and inspiration to our readers.

It is sold with the understanding that the publisher and the individual authors are not engaged in the rendering of psychological, legal, accounting, or other professional advice. The content and views in each chapter are the sole expression and opinion of its author and not necessarily the views of Christie Ruffino, Unleashed Publishing, or the Seven Figure Book Launch Joint Venture.

For more information, contact:
Unleashed Publishing
A division of Christie Lee LLC
www.ChristieRuffino.com

Printed in the United States of America

ISBN: 978-1-939794-37-6

Table of Contents

Dedication

This book is dedicated to those who feel the quiet pull toward something more, even when the path ahead is unclear, and the courage to begin feels fragile.

To the entrepreneurs who build not just for income, but for meaning.

To the visionaries who choose purpose over permission.

It is for the leaders who know their work was never meant to be small.

For the creators who refuse to trade their calling for comfort.

To those who continue to rise, even when they are misunderstood, doubted, or walking alone. To those who continue to rise, even when they are misunderstood, doubted, or walking alone. And to the few who are brave enough to listen to the voice within them that says, “There is more for you,” and take action.

Most importantly, it is dedicated to the remarkable contributors in these pages who shared their truth with courage, generosity, and heart, so that others may recognize themselves, rise into their purpose, and answer the call they were born to live.

The Power of a Story

At the heart of every purpose-driven life is the impact we leave behind and the legacy we choose to build. Long after achievements fade and milestones are forgotten, what remains is who we became, who we lifted, and the truth we were brave enough to live out loud. Each of us carries a story that was never meant to stay hidden, the blueprint of our becoming, shaped by experiences no one else could walk and wisdom no one else could earn.

Your story is not random. It is encoded with insight, clarity, and a sense of calling. When embraced and shared, it becomes more than a memory; it becomes a mirror, a permission slip, and an invitation for others to rise. No one else can deliver the message your life has been forming, and without it, the world is missing a voice that could shift perspectives, awaken courage, and change trajectories.

The ability to own and express your story is one of your greatest assets. True influence is not rooted in performance or perfection, but in authenticity and alignment. When the right story is shared at the right time, it opens doors, builds trust, and creates momentum beyond a single moment, creating a ripple effect that multiplies purpose, clarity, and impact.

For more than a decade, I have walked beside entrepreneurs, leaders, and visionaries as they reclaimed their stories and stepped into their calling. I have seen lives realign, businesses transform, and confidence rise when someone stops hiding what shaped them and begins leading with it. Story is not simply something you tell; it is something you become.

Embrace your story. It holds the key to your next chapter and the legacy you were created to leave.

Power to you and to the story only you can tell!

"What lies behind us and what lies before us
are tiny matters compared to what lies within us."

—Ralph Waldo Emerson

Introduction

Genius Unleashed is the second volume in the *Unleashed Series*, a body of work created for those who sense they were designed for more than survival, more than success, and more than simply "doing well." This series was born from decades of walking beside entrepreneurs, leaders, and visionaries who carry something meaningful inside them, yet often find themselves living beneath their assignment.

Long before this series existed, the stories came first. Through twelve #1 bestselling volumes in the *Overcoming Mediocrity* collection, through our *Mastery Unleashed* podcast, and through years of coaching and publishing leaders into their next chapter, one truth became impossible to ignore: extraordinary people are quietly underexpressed in a world that needs them more than ever.

There comes a moment in every purpose-driven life when the noise finally quiets enough for a deeper voice to be heard. It is not the voice of pressure, productivity, or fear disguised as responsibility. It is the voice that says there is more for you, and you were created for it. If you are holding this book, something within you already knows that the way you have been working, building, and giving no longer fits who you are becoming. You have outgrown the version of yourself that merely survives. You are being called into the version of yourself that leads.

That transition rarely arrives through comfort. More often, it begins quietly, in the exhaustion no one sees, in the frustration of doing everything right and still feeling behind, in the subtle grief of knowing your gifts are larger than the containers you have been placing them in. You are not broken. You are not behind. You are not unqualified. You are waking up.

Genius does not arrive gently. It awakens after something collapses. It reveals itself when old strategies stop working and familiar structures no longer hold. What you may have labeled burnout, disruption, or delay may in truth have been your initiation into the next level of your calling. The men and women whose stories fill these pages did not reach their clarity through comfort. They reached it through courage, obedience, reinvention, and the willingness to answer the quiet nudge that said, *"This is not all you are here to do."*

Each story you are about to read is not simply inspirational. It is instructional at the level of identity. These are not tales of perfection. They are living evidence of what happens when a person finally chooses to stop shrinking, stop postponing their purpose, and stop negotiating with the life they were created to live. And because transformation is meant to be supported, not admired from a distance, every expert featured in this book has also extended a personal invitation to you. Along with their story, each contributor is offering a valuable, complimentary resource designed to help you go deeper, take your next step with clarity, and apply what resonates most directly to your own journey toward impact, purpose, and legacy.

Every chapter is a mirror. A mirror of what happens when someone stops shrinking. A mirror of what happens when obedience replaces approval. A mirror of what happens when survival gives way to sovereignty. A mirror of what happens when a person chooses purpose over permission.

As you read, you may feel something begin to rise that has little to do with motivation and everything to do with remembrance. A knowing. A clarity. A quiet but unshakable sense that your life is meant to carry more meaning, more influence, and more impact than it currently does. Your genius has never been missing. It has been waiting for you to become ready to lead with it.

This book was written for the moment you decide to answer that call. It exists to meet you at the threshold between where you have been and who you are becoming. It invites you to step into the work you were created to do, to build the purpose-driven business that reflects your truth, and to create an impact that extends far beyond your own success.

You are not here to construct something that drains your spirit. You are here to build something that expresses who you truly are. You are not here to chase success. You are here to embody significance.

This book is your threshold.

Cross it.

Your genius is ready.

Christie Ruffino

A Morning That Changed Everything

The first thing I noticed was wetness, not from tears I remembered crying, but from the pillow beneath my cheek, soaked. Sunlight was beginning to creep through the blinds in thin, defiant streaks, like it had no business shining into a world that felt so dark.

I sat up slowly, disoriented, heavy. It was the first time in weeks that I had slept more than a few hours, and the weight of everything I had been carrying hit me the second I opened my eyes. My stomach growled, reminding me that groceries were low again. But worse than hunger was the tight, choking panic that had become my morning ritual.

I had been scammed. Not just a little. I had lost my *entire* life savings in what I believed would be the investment that would finally set me free. It was supposed to be my ticket to freedom. Freedom from the poverty mindset I inherited, from the anxious hustle of barely scraping by, from always being the one figuring it out for everyone else, *except myself.*

But freedom didn't come. Not then. Instead, the walls closed in around me like a vice, tightening with every unpaid bill and broken promise.

I was months behind on rent. My credit cards were maxed. My business accounts were a mess. And I had no idea how I'd pay back the friends who had so generously loaned me money just to keep the lights on and cover the software subscriptions that powered what was left of my business.

And yet… that morning was different because I had a dream.

Not just any dream; a vivid, unforgettable one. In it, I was talking with Cathy, a friend and fellow coach. I was spilling it all; the shame, the fear, the disbelief that someone like me, with so much business experience, had ended up here. She listened quietly and then said one thing that jolted me awake:

"I don't know how to help you, Christie… but I know someone who might be able to. Do you know Tom Matzen?"

The name landed like lightning. I sat up in bed, instantly alert, heart pounding, mind racing.

It was early, only 7:30 am for me on the East Coast in Florida, but I didn't hesitate. With shaky hands, I grabbed my phone and typed out a Facebook message to Tom. I didn't even know what I was asking for, or if he'd even remember who I was. I just knew I had no options left. Out of pride. Out of time. Within minutes, he responded.

A few hours later, we were on a call. I didn't tell him about the dream. I was afraid he'd think I was nuts. But I told him everything else: how I was drowning, how I had nothing left but hope and a stubborn refusal to give up. I knew he'd ridden the entrepreneurial rollercoaster, too, and maybe, just maybe, he could offer some light in the fog I was stuck in.

Tom didn't offer pity. He offered a partnership.

That call became the catalyst for what would later evolve into the **Seven Figure Book Launch Program**, and the moment I stopped waiting to be rescued, and started rewriting the story of my life.

The crazy part? It wasn't until a few days later that I discovered the truth: Cathy and Tom didn't even know each other. They had never met. Not in person. Not online. Not at all.

That's when it hit me, this wasn't just a dream. It was a divine breadcrumb. A whisper from God. A message meant specifically for me. And I had a choice: I could dismiss it, chalk it up to exhaustion and stress… or I could trust it, even if I didn't fully understand it.

When Experience Isn't Enough: The High Cost of Getting It Wrong

I've always had an entrepreneurial spirit. It was just wired into me.

As a kid, I remember my grandmother paying my brother, cousin, and me to pick up sticks in her front yard. Most kids would do the job, grab their cash, and blow it on candy at the corner store. And I did buy candy, but then I sold it to the kids in her neighborhood for a profit. That was my first taste of leverage, though I wouldn't have known to call it that back then. I didn't just want candy. I wanted the possibility.

Growing up, money was always tight. My mom raised us on pennies. And that scarcity wasn't just about what was (or wasn't) in the bank; it was a mindset. A constant, gnawing worry. A belief that there wouldn't be enough. Enough food. Enough time. Enough security. And for a long time, I carried that mindset into adulthood.

I married a man with a vision to start an auto repair business. I jumped in with both feet and helped him grow that one idea into a thriving company with multiple locations. I didn't just believe in his dream, I *built* it with him. But when our marriage ended, so did my role in that business. I had poured so much of myself into something that no longer belonged to me, and suddenly I found myself at a crossroads: starting over as a single mom, without a roadmap, without income, and with a deep need for stability.

So, I got a job. Not just any job, I became a branch manager at a staffing company. It paid well. It offered flexibility. It allowed me to tap into my leadership and sales skills. On the outside, it looked like I had landed on my feet. But inside, I felt like I was just... existing.

Because deep down, I knew I wasn't meant to climb someone else's ladder. I wasn't made to be boxed in by time clocks and cubicles. I had ideas. I had ambition. I had this relentless pull to build something of my own.

That's when I started a women's networking group in a Chicago suburb to bring together like-minded businesswomen. But that one group grew. And grew. And split into two groups. They both grew and split into more.

Before long, I was leading a women's referral network with chapters across the United States. That 23-year journey changed everything. I found purpose. I found passion. I found *power* in building community and helping other women rise. And it was that success story—*of going from near-bankruptcy to leading a national movement*—that opened the door to something unexpected: Publishing.

In 2012, I was invited to share my story in a collaborative book, and when it launched... something clicked. I saw how powerful it was to use a book not just as a business card, but as a transformational tool. I realized storytelling was more than a way to inspire; it was a strategy. And so, I launched my own publishing company to help entrepreneurs and business leaders share their stories, amplify their messages, and build authority with a book.

I thought I had finally found "it." My zone of genius. My true path.

But what most people didn't see was the "Wizard behind the curtain," pulling levers, spinning wheels, trying desperately to keep the illusion of success alive. On the outside, everything looked polished and powerful. But behind the scenes? I was scrambling. Tired. Overwhelmed. Stuck in a cycle that was anything but magical.

The Truth Behind the Curtain

I was trying every strategy imaginable to grow my coaching and publishing business. Funnel after funnel. Course after course. Challenge after challenge. I hired mentors, joined masterminds, bought programs that promised to unlock the "six-figure secret." And while they kept me busy and even got me clients, none of them created consistent results. I had cash flow, but it came with a never-ending rollercoaster of hope and frustration. Some months, I'd make a lot of money. Others, I could barely keep the lights on.

I was tired. Tired of the hustle. Tired of being in constant creation mode. Tired of trying to be a tech expert, a marketing guru, a social media strategist, a copywriter, a publishing expert, an accountant, and a coach, *all at once.*

What I really wanted was to serve. To coach. To lead. To help people win in business without burning out or going broke trying to figure it out. But I couldn't seem to escape the grind.

Even more troubling than that was my client's success. Or should I say lack of. They were always so proud of the new book we helped them create. And I was proud, too… until the excitement faded and reality set in. We'd get picture after picture of them holding their new literary masterpieces, only to hear back from them months later as their frustration increased because their new book didn't move the needle in their business.

And then along came the investment opportunity.

It looked like the perfect solution, and the way out of that exhausting cycle. I could finally afford to hire the right coach and build a team to help me with marketing, social media, and other tasks that had worn me down. I was very excited.

It was highly recommended by a friend, packaged beautifully, sold with certainty, and ticked every box on the "freedom" checklist. So, I trusted. I said yes. I put in all I had left, financially and emotionally, because it promised substantial dividends and a reasonably quick and lucrative payout. I thought it was a no-brainer opportunity.

But I lost everything.

And that was the moment everything came crashing down.

The financial loss was devastating. But the emotional aftermath was worse. I felt humiliated. Ashamed. Stupid, even. How could someone like me, with decades of experience, three six-figure businesses under my belt, and a reputation for helping others succeed, have fallen for it?

The old scarcity mindset came rushing back with a vengeance. I found myself spiraling into depression. My confidence took a massive hit. I stopped showing up fully in my business. My energy was off. I could feel it, and I'm sure everyone else could too. The harder I tried to pretend everything was fine and push through, the more stuck I felt.

There were days I couldn't even afford groceries. Days I had to borrow money just to put gas in my car. Days I wondered if it would be easier to just give up. But something in me wouldn't let that happen. Because despite everything, somewhere deep down, I still believed I was meant for more.

That belief, even when it felt like a whisper, kept me going. I clung to faith. I clung to hope. I clung to the idea that maybe, just maybe, this rock bottom moment was happening for me… not to me. And eventually, that whisper turned into a wake-up call, *literally.*

A dream that felt like a message from God.

A conversation with a trusted friend, who led me (in the dream) to someone I had only briefly known, someone who would become the co-creator of the next chapter of my business… and my life. That moment didn't just change my thinking; it rerouted my life.

Because I realized I wasn't alone in this. There were so many others like me—*smart, experienced, heart-centered entrepreneurs*—who were stuck on that same hamster wheel, working tirelessly but not getting ahead. People who were tired of overpromising coaches, endless upsells, and broken business models.

That's when it became crystal clear: I wasn't meant just to survive this. I was meant to solve this. And that's what I set out to do.

Desperation, Surrender… and a Divine Nudge

It was just a dream.

The moment I woke up, I knew it was more than that. It was different. Vivid. Timed too perfectly to be a coincidence. Just four days prior, I shared my situation with my small group from Church, and they prayed for me. I'm pretty private. I don't usually share. But I was so emotionally wrecked that week, I completely broke down and let it all out.

I had been clinging to pride, to control, to the belief that I had to figure it all out on my own. But now? I was done pretending. If I didn't reach out, if I didn't *ask for help*, nothing would change, and the weight of that truth was unbearable.

That morning, with shaky hands and zero expectations, I messaged Tom. And that tiny act of obedience… became the turning point of everything.

Making a Decision, and Making That Decision Right

After that call with Tom, something inside me reignited. It wasn't just hope, it was direction.

We talked again the next day. He had ideas. I had experience. And between us, something sparked that neither of us could ignore. That was the birth of what would become the **Seven Figure Book Launch Program.** It wasn't just a new offer, but a completely different way of doing business.

Finally, I had a model that aligned with what I always believed: that coaches and experts should *earn* their clients' trust through results, not just promises.

This wasn't a handout. I still had no money. I was still in survival mode. So I did what I've always done when things get tough: I went all in.

I said yes to the partnership before I had "proof" it would work. I brought to the table everything I had built over the years: my publishing background, my marketing experience, my deep understanding of personal branding and storytelling, and began building again, this time with a foundation rooted in collaboration, integrity, and results.

I stopped wasting time on endless marketing tactics that didn't work. I leaned into my strengths: strategy, structure, visibility, and implementation. I focused on creating a clear, results-based offer and on serving deeply, rather than chasing everyone. I showed up every day, even when I was scared, even when I was unsure. Even when my bank account said I had no business believing in big things. And that's when the momentum came.

Because success doesn't come from getting everything right, it comes from choosing to rise—*again and again*—and becoming someone qualified through the climb, not in spite of it.

The High Cost of Figuring It Out Alone

The moment I said yes to rebuilding wasn't the moment everything got easy. It was just the moment I stopped sinking.

I'd love to say things clicked into place immediately. That the partnership with Tom took off overnight, or that my new offer filled up with clients right away. But that would be a lie. What really happened was this: I walked straight into the weeds. Again.

You see, I'd already spent years trying to build something sustainable. I had invested thousands into programs, coaches, online tools, and masterminds. I tried all the strategies: launching courses, creating memberships, writing email funnels, running challenges, building out value ladders, and sales pages. You name it, I did it.

Each time, I thought: *Maybe this will be the thing.*

Sometimes, I'd even get a few wins: a new client, a solid month of revenue, a little boost of momentum. But then? Crickets. The pipeline would dry up. I'd be back at square one. I kept hopping from one idea to the next, hoping something would finally stick.

The truth? Most of what I tried just kept me busy… not profitable. I wasn't building a business, I was building a burnout. And burnout doesn't scale.

The most heartbreaking part? I saw the same thing happening to other women around me. Brilliant coaches. Experts with heart, talent, and life-changing skills, stuck in the same cycle. Following formulas that worked for their coach, but not for them. Being told to push harder. To "trust the process." To invest again and again in programs that had no skin in the game.

And when those programs didn't deliver? The shame fell on the student.

I wasn't failing because I wasn't trying. I was failing because the industry was broken. It rewarded marketing more than mastery. Style over substance. Visibility over value.

When Tom and I started building the Seven Figure Book Launch Program, I knew I couldn't repeat those mistakes. I had to get honest about what didn't work, not just for me, but for the hundreds of women I'd watched struggle, too. So we started stripping everything back.

I let go of the *"Ascension Model"*; the never-ending funnel of freebie to tripwire to low-ticket course to upsell to upsell to upsell. I dropped the bells and whistles, the shiny objects, and the guru-style sales scripts.

Instead, I focused on three simple things:

1. One clear, transformational high-ticket offer.
2. One specific, right-fit client.
3. One consistent method for enrolling them through aligned visibility and authority.

That simplicity was hard. It forced me to let go of the complexity I had spent years building. But it also gave me clarity, and finally, traction. Still, even with this clarity, I had to do the work of refining my own beliefs.

I had to rebuild trust in myself and in the idea that business didn't have to be so hard. I had to learn how to lead from value, not volume. I had to get really good at saying "no" to things that didn't align, even if they looked promising on the outside.

It took time. It took falling down, *more than once.* It took learning how to structure programs that *actually got people results,* not just ones that sold well. It took building systems, creating duplicatable processes, and developing a framework that could be customized and scaled without crumbling.

I've lived through the failed launches. I've endured offers that flopped. I've implemented ideas that looked great in theory but tanked in practice. But each one taught me something important. And most importantly, each one brought me to believe in a new way of doing business. With a system that helps our clients avoid those same weeds and collapse their timelines rather than extend them.

That's what makes our program different.

We didn't build it from theory. We built it from the dirt. From the missteps. From the heartbreak. From the "almosts." From the "this should've worked" moments that didn't.

Over the years, we both tested. We failed. We adjusted. We earned every lesson. And that's why I can look any expert in the eye and say, *"If you're coachable, committed, and ready to stop guessing, we've got you."*

I've been where they are, I've walked through the weeds, and now, I know the way out.

Slaying the Chaos with Simplicity, Story, and Strategy

The journey through the weeds didn't just give me battle scars, it gave me a proven strategy.

I stopped being the woman who tried to do it all. I became the woman who focused on what actually moved the needle. That shift, from scattered to strategic, is when my *genius was finally unleashed.* It was no longer buried under burnout and busywork. It became the foundation for everything that followed.

I stopped hustling for every sale and started attracting the right clients by leading with clarity, confidence, and *authority.* I became a better entrepreneur, but more importantly, I became the kind of guide I always needed.

I know what it's like to follow all the rules and still fall short. I know what it feels like to invest everything and still feel stuck. And now? I know exactly what it takes to rise.

Through this work, I developed systems. I learned how to structure offers that guarantee client results. I built an enrollment process that is values-driven instead of pressure-driven. I became an expert in building visibility with intention, not noise. I built teams, streamlined operations, and started teaching my clients how to do the same, without the burnout.

If you're stuck in the grind, wondering if this is all there is, here are the three truths I wish someone had handed me before I burned it all down.

1. One Client

Get radically clear on who you serve. You can't help everyone, but you can create massive results for the right person. The clearer your niche, the stronger your message and the easier your sales. And regardless of how narrow you think your niche is, and that you'll be leaving people behind, we live in a world of abundance with hundreds, if not thousands, of people just like your right-fit client whose life you could change in a massive way.

2. One Offer

Stop splitting your focus. Build one high-impact, high-ticket program that delivers undeniable transformation. When you simplify your business model, you amplify your income—*and your impac*t—and become known as the King/Queen of XYZ, making you the sought-after industry expert who is highly paid and easily referable.

3. One Core Message

Your story is your greatest sales tool. When you lead with the truth of *why* you do what you do—*and how you've earned the right to lead*—you'll connect with your audience in a way no script ever could.

These are the very principles I used to rebuild my business, and they're the foundation of how I help others scale theirs. Because when you stop spinning and start simplifying, you stop surviving… and start leading.

This Isn't Just My Story: It's Yours Too

Today, my life and business look nothing like they did during those long, heavy mornings filled with fear and uncertainty.

Now, I wake up with clarity. With systems in place. With a lean, empowered team. With a simple, repeatable structure that allows me to operate in my zone of genius: serving clients, creating impact, and doing work that actually matters.

No more chasing clients. No more guessing what to do next. No more overdelivering in underpaying programs. I've built a business that's both profitable and purposeful, and most importantly, duplicatable.

We have a clear calendar. We know exactly when we're launching. Our partners are aligned. Our offers are proven. And our clients? They're no longer drowning in a sea of strategy. They're finally getting results; real, sustainable, life-changing results.

That's what lights me up the most. Because this isn't just my story anymore, it's ours.

If you're reading this and feeling that tug—*the one that whispers you were made for more*—I want you to know: you're not crazy. You're not behind. And you're not alone.

You're standing at your own lightbulb moment, just like I was.

Your story doesn't end in the weeds. Not if you don't want it to. And if you're ready to stop guessing and start growing a business that works, one that actually pays you well, gives you time back, and serves from your soul, we've built something just for you.

The **Seven Figure Book Launch Program** isn't just a course. It's a collaboration. It's a proven path to turn your story, your expertise, and your message into a client-attracting movement backed by a risk-reversed model that proves we're in this with you.

Your next chapter is calling.

Your story is waiting. Your offer is waiting. Your *genius* is waiting to be *unleashed.* And when it is, your message won't just resonate… it will ripple.

I'd be honored to help you clarify it, write it, and live it.

Christie Ruffino

Christie Ruffino knows firsthand what it's like to face challenges that feel impossible to overcome, yet she did. Instead of asking, "Why me?" she leaned into "What's next?" and turned her mess into her mission. That journey led her to discover her true purpose: helping entrepreneurs build a seven-figure business by leveraging their wisdom and a great business book.

She's the founder of Mastery Unleashed Coaching™ and co-creator of the Seven Figure Book Launch Program, where she helps coaches and industry experts package their brilliance into high-impact offers and bestselling books that don't just elevate their brand but guarantee results.

With over three decades of entrepreneurial experience, Christie has worked with more than 3,000 women, helping them grow their revenue through clarity, collaboration, and strategic visibility. She's a best-selling author with

20 books, a certified John Maxwell coach, and a student of icons like Bob Burg, Jack Canfield, and Larry Winget. Her work has been featured on Inc. com, WGN Radio, and NBC's The Morning Blend.

She's also the host of a top-rated podcast, an international speaker, and a firm believer that business should be both profitable and purpose-driven.

Christie is an avid reader, a serial smart ass, and a proud grandma of the two most adorable kids ever (with thousands of photos to prove it). When she's not helping entrepreneurs build businesses that fund their legacy, she can usually be found cruising triple-digit speeds down open country roads on her 1,700 cc Harley Davidson Streetglide (skydiving is still a hard no), or being bossed around by Missy, her fearless MinPin sidekick. Missy is the unfiltered inspiration behind Christie's popular Missy Unleashed, followed by more than 500 fans who come for the humor and stay for the surprisingly spot-on business, life, and legacy lessons.

Christie Ruffino
Mastery Unleashed Coaching
www.ChristieRuffino.com

The Seven Figure Shift™ Coach: Your AI-Powered Unstoppable Game Plan

Stuck at 5 or 6 figures? Want a clear, executable plan that tells you exactly what to focus on—without guesswork or overwhelm?? Get The Seven Figure Shift™ Coach FREE.

Build a clear path from ambition to execution. The Seven Figure Shift™ Coach GPT helps you set bold targets, install resilient habits, and map a simple roadmap that compounds results in your business and life. You will clarify what matters, remove what doesn't, and lock in the next right moves so progress is inevitable.

https://SevenFigureShift.com/sfsc-genius-unleashed-book

Dr. Tammy De Mirza

When Spirit Said Stay: Rising Sovereign From the Edge of Everything

The Pain

"You want me to stay… don't you?"

The Florida air was thick that day, heavy with the kind of humidity that clings to your skin and makes even breathing feel like an effort. Outside, the sun painted everything in golden light. Inside that small, borrowed house, I was drowning.

The bathroom was the only place that gave me comfort. As an adult, whenever life hurt more than I could hold, I would turn to the tub. The warmth of the water softened what felt hard and unforgiving. It had been my sanctuary for years, the place I went when I couldn't figure things out, when I needed to feel held by something even if no one else was holding me.

I turned the faucet on full and let the tub fill slowly, the echo of water hitting porcelain a sharp contrast to the silence inside of me. My thoughts were loud. Accusatory. Deafening. **I had nothing left.**

No home.

No job.

No money.

Not even a bed that was truly mine to sleep in. I had lost my furniture, my savings, my sense of safety. I was rotating between borrowed spaces, my car, and the kindness of others, with only my clothes and a fractured spirit to my name. There were days I had fifty cents in my checking account and couldn't afford a hamburger at McDonald's.

I was homeless, hopeless, and deeply ashamed.

I had trusted a man, a smooth talker with grand visions, who turned out to be a Bernie Madoff clone. But the most painful part was knowing I had felt the warning signs from the beginning. My intuition had whispered. My body had tightened. My senses had told me the truth, and I had denied it all.

I climbed into the tub slowly, the warmth wrapping around me like a familiar embrace that this time couldn't quite reach the depth of my despair. This was the moment I finally accepted what had happened: I had lost everything. I had been conned. And somewhere along the way, I had abandoned the woman who always knew better.

The thought rose up quietly, almost logically:

Maybe I've gone as far as I can in this life.

Maybe the only thing left to do is leave.

I knew exactly how I could end my life. The plan was clear in my mind, not for that night, but soon. I would do it here, in the one place that had always held me. The decision to end my life was born in that bathtub, in the moment I fully realized how far I had fallen and how responsible I felt for every step. And yet, even in that darkness, love insisted on one last act.

Before I carried out my plan, I decided I would visit the four people who meant the most to me, my children, my best friend, and a man I'd been working with. One person at a time, to share the last moments and memories. One final visit each. They would never know these were goodbyes. I would simply show up, love them, and let my presence be a quiet thank-you for the role they'd played in my life.

The first visit was planned for the very next morning. I got out of the tub, dried off, got dressed, and walked out to my car. As I backed out of the driveway, numb and resigned, my phone buzzed. *"I just wired you $1,300."* It was from my best friend, Robyn. I froze. *"$1,300?"* I stared at the screen, heart racing. It was such an oddly specific amount. Unexpected. Precise. It cut through the fog like a beam of light.

And then I felt it, not a voice in my ear, but a knowing deep in my spirit: **You're not done.**

I pulled the car back into the garage, shut off the engine, and sat there in stunned silence as tears began to fall. I walked back into the house and called Robyn. When she answered, everything in me broke open.

"You have no idea what you just stopped," I whispered, and I confessed. Robyn and I cried together. She had no idea what I had been planning, yet she acted on a nudge to send that exact amount at that exact moment.

Within two minutes of hanging up, my son called. He didn't know why, he just "felt something." Two minutes after that, my daughter called with the same unease. None of them knew what I had planned. But on a soul level, they knew.

Something spiritual, something supernatural was happening. The timing was too precise, the alignment too exact to chalk it up to coincidence. The universe had intercepted my death. Not because I was special, but because I had work to do.

If I was going to stay, I knew one thing with absolute clarity: **I could no longer deny who I truly am.**

Flashback to the Pain Origin

"You don't just wake up ready to die unless something inside of you has been dying for years."

People say pain shapes us. I believe pain buries us. And if we don't learn how to resurrect, it quietly becomes our identity.

My story didn't begin in that bathtub in Florida. It began decades earlier, in a house that felt more like a battlefield than a home.

I was eleven years old when everything changed.

A Southern Baptist pastor had visited my grandmother's house. He spoke of love, heaven, and hell. I didn't want to hear about hellfire or fear, but I still prayed the prayer, not because I was afraid of punishment, but because I was desperate for love. Real, safe love was not something I had known. My grandmother was abusive. My mother, too. That house was layered with tension, volatility, and emotional landmines.

The next morning, I woke up… different. I knew things. Felt things. I could hear my mother's thoughts from the other room. I knew what my father was going to say before he opened his mouth. I saw, without being physically present in her room, that my older sister was still in bed and knew exactly what trouble was coming if she didn't get up for school. It was like being plugged into a grid no one had told me existed.

At eleven years old, I could see into people's bodies, read energy, and access knowledge that hadn't been taught to me. I later learned there were names for these abilities:

- **Clairvoyance**—clear seeing
- **Clairaudience**—clear hearing
- **Clairscent**—clear smelling
- **Clairgustance**—clear tasting
- **Clairsentience**—clear feeling

They were my Sensory Superpowers™. But at the time, they felt like a threat.

This was the South. The Bible Belt. A culture where someone like me would be either worshipped or feared. I made people uncomfortable without knowing why. So, I did what gifted children often do when the world isn't ready for them:

I hid.

I learned to hide my abilities.

I hid my truth.

I hid my pain.

It became second nature.

Fast forward a few years. I was in my early twenties, newly married, a young mom, heavily involved in a mega-church. I had a lot of visibility there. I played Mary in the Passion Play, sang on stage, and did TV segments. On the outside, I looked like I had found my place. Inside, I was exhausted and cracking.

One day, a man walked into my house, and without thinking, I scanned his body. I told him he had cancer in his right lung and how long he had been told he had to live. It was as automatic to me as breathing. He walked out of my home cancer-free, and the tests later proved his healing.

Soon after, I began laying hands on people. They were healed. Every. Single. One.

I told them not to talk about it. I didn't want the attention. But word spread anyway. People started showing up at my house at all hours. They woke me in the middle of the night. They asked for healing, for prayer, for answers, for more than I had the capacity to give.

And I gave it. Again and again. Until I had nothing left.

Behind the miracle stories was a private torment no one saw. My first husband was later diagnosed with multiple conditions that made daily life chaotic and emotionally unsafe. I was gaslit, emotionally battered, and constantly made to question my own sanity. I could help others heal, but I couldn't find a way to rescue myself.

I did what many wounded empaths do when the weight of the world becomes too much: I shut it all down. I told God, *"Get them away from me. I cannot carry the weight of other people's pain anymore. If you think I'll ever be mature enough to handle this again, bring it back. But for now, I'm done."*

And with that, the gifts went into the background of my existence. The abilities went quiet. I stopped praying. I stopped saying God's name. I built a life that looked successful. I started a business. Bought a condo. Became the first woman in my family to do it all on her own. On the outside, I was thriving. On the inside, I was still fractured.

At thirty-eight, something significant happened with a friend that opened the door again. The abilities returned, slowly at first, then intensely. The visions. The inner voice. The knowing. My Sensory Superpowers quietly came back online.

After thirteen years of suppressing them, I didn't trust myself to openly embrace them. I struggled like every other human does when they suddenly start experiencing supernatural things they cannot fathom, much less explain.

I questioned every feeling, every message, every intuitive nudge. I was terrified I was making it all up, terrified that maybe I really was crazy.

The irony? I was more afraid of my own power than I was of other people's betrayal… And betrayal did come.

I entered marriages without using discernment, and after leaving one husband who was emotionally unavailable due to a personality disorder, I met someone new. He seemed like such a great spiritual fit for me, but the spiritual conviction, knowing, and ease with which he spoke of it was instead a facade that I would later find out the truth about. He also introduced me to a very charismatic, confident, and charming man who said all the right things to get me to invest with him. And I, still doubting my inner compass, followed.

My intuition kept whispering, *"Something isn't right."* I ignored it.

That choice led me straight into the deepest pit of my life.

He was a conman. A Bernie Madoff type. He stole nearly everything, my money, my sense of safety, and what little remained of my self-trust.

I became homeless, not just spiritually, but literally. The woman who used to help others find healing now didn't know where she'd sleep next.

I moved into a borrowed home in Florida. My bank account dissolved. No job. No income. My furniture was gone. My future felt erased. I had failed at marriage. I was penniless, so I failed at keeping myself safe. And worst of all, failed to listen to the one voice that had never lied to me: my own.

That's when the bathtub happened. That's when I decided, *"This is the end."* But the end I was planning was not the end the universe had in mind.

Robyn's text. My children's calls. The timing. The precision. The unmistakable spiritual orchestration. It wasn't just about stopping my death. It was about awakening my life.

Everything I had endured was not random. It was the curriculum, a soul-initiated rite of passage to become the guide I was always meant to be. The truth was, I was never broken. I was never crazy. I was never too much. **I was powerful.** And I had forgotten.

The Lightbulb Moment

"The only way out is to do the opposite of everything you've done until now."

Sitting in that dark garage, phone in hand, heart pounding, I knew one thing: I was meant to stay. But staying couldn't just mean surviving. Staying had to mean transforming.

No more disowning my abilities.

No more silencing my Clairsenses to make others comfortable.

No more ignoring the inner warnings that had always tried to protect me.

No more shrinking to be acceptable.

If I continued living the way I had—*denying myself, doubting my knowing, abandoning my truth*—I would die slowly anyway.

So, I made a vow in that garage:

I will rise. And I will teach others how to rise, too.

What Moved Me Through the Pain

"This time, I wouldn't be rescued. I would rise."

Once I chose to stay, I knew I could never go back to the life I had built before. That life had been meticulously constructed, yes, but on a foundation of denial, people-pleasing, and survival. If I was going to rebuild, it had to be from truth.

The first step was radical responsibility. I looked at my life—*the betrayal, the bankruptcy, the homelessness*—and I said, *"I chose this. I attracted this. Now I can choose differently."* I returned to the spiritual tools I had once put on the shelf.

I dusted off **The Breakthrough Code™**, which had been given to me when I was only thirteen, a five-step process that guides people through deep transformation. Later, I received an alchemy process I now call the **Breakthrough Manifestation Code™**. It was this process that I used to walk myself out of homelessness and that I now use to teach clients how to manifest miracles "out of thin air" as conscious alchemists.

At this point, I used it on myself every single day.

I confronted my limiting beliefs.

I exposed my patterns.

I released subconscious contracts with suffering, scarcity, and self-betrayal.

It wasn't glamorous. I didn't manifest mansions overnight. What I manifested were lessons, tests, cycles, and triggers, each one giving me another opportunity to respond differently. Instead of asking, *"Why is this happening to me?"* I began asking, *"What is this trying to teach me?"*

There were moments when I had literally fifty cents in my bank account and no idea how I would eat. I was still relying on borrowed spaces and short-term arrangements. But through the Breakthrough Manifestation Code™, which was divinely given to me to overcome my life's predicaments,

I began to see real evidence that the universe was responding when I aligned.

I manifested:

- Meals when I had no money for food.
- A bed when I had nowhere to sleep.
- Clients right when I needed to pay for gas, bills, or groceries.
- Supernatural and sudden gifts of money from people guided to help me, like Robyn.

I was learning conscious alchemy, turning pain into power, shame into sovereignty, fear into faith. And the more I embodied it, the more my life began to shift.

The very tools that were carrying me out of homelessness and despair became the same tools I began using with clients. They experienced quantum shifts in health, abundance, career breakthroughs, and relationships.

From homeless and hopeless, I became clear, confident, and in command.

For the first time in my life, I didn't just believe in my power. **I embodied it.**

From the Weeds to the Way Forward

"I knew how to help others create miracles, but I didn't yet know how to build a thriving, global business around that genius."

After I recommitted to my path, a part of me assumed the rest would be easy.

I had the tools.

I had the gifts.

I had the testimony.

But knowing how to create miracles and knowing how to create a sustainable, scalable business are not the same thing.

At first, I repeated an old pattern. I would manifest money, then watch it slip away. Opportunities came and evaporated. I cycled through what I now call the empath loop: Give. Help. Crash. Recover. Repeat.

One day, I felt like a powerful healer. The next, I was on the floor, wondering if I had made it all up. It was like trying to build a cathedral on quicksand. Eventually, I knew I had to stop patching cracks and pour a new foundation.

I spent seven full days in silence, journaling, meditating, listening. No distractions. No noise. Just me, my patterns, and the presence of something greater.

In that silence, I uncovered a belief that had been running me for years:

That being a powerful intuitive meant I had to suffer.

That charging money for spiritual work was wrong.

That success would make people resent me.

That to be worthy, I had to sacrifice myself continually.

Using The Breakthrough Code™, I went after those roots with intention. I confronted the spiritual contracts I had made with suffering. I released the guilt around being powerful, wealthy, and seen.

Something shifted. Within days, I signed my first high-ticket client. She didn't just pay. She transformed. She experienced emotional breakthroughs, clarity of purpose, and a financial windfall that surprised both of us. That one client validated years of inner work and showed me what was possible when I aligned my power and my pricing. But there was another layer.

I realized that if I wanted to serve globally, I had to treat my calling like the powerful business it was meant to be. Being gifted was not enough.

I began seeking out world-class mentors, speakers, and strategists. Over time, I invested more than **$1.5 million in my growth**, coaches, masterminds, business architects, spiritual teachers, and performance experts.

I wasn't buying quick fixes. I was building infrastructure around my genius. I learned marketing, messaging, and offers that honored the depth of my work. I learned how to create containers that could hold the level of transformation my clients were experiencing. I learned to combine intuitive intelligence with aligned strategy. I stopped seeing myself as "just" a healer or "just" an intuitive.

I began to see myself as what I truly am: A clairscendent leader who moves between worlds—*spiritual and practical, energetic and tangible*—bridging them for the sake of real, measurable change.

Slowly, my work expanded far beyond that small borrowed house in Florida. Clients began finding me across the country, then around the world. My business stopped feeling like a constant test and began to feel like what it truly is: **A sacred vessel for transformation.**

If I could go back and change one thing, it would be this: I would have asked for support sooner. You cannot rise sovereign by yourself.

Sovereignty isn't isolation. It's alignment. It's guidance. It's being willing to be seen, and held, as you become who you were always meant to be.

That's why I walk beside my clients now. I know the weeds. I know the loneliness of wandering without a map. And I know the miracle that waits on the other side of the work.

Dragon Strategies: Becoming the Fire

"I didn't just slay the dragon, I became the fire."

My rise didn't come from one big moment. It came from repeated, sovereign choices.

I stopped waiting to be rescued.

I stopped apologizing for my power.

I stopped denying my Sensory Superpowers™.

I began building the version of me I had always sensed was there, the sovereign version. I immersed myself in energy systems, subconscious programming, and universal and spiritual laws. I studied the language of the clairsenses and how they interface with high-level decision-making, leadership, and wealth creation. I didn't just use these tools, I mastered them.

My spiritual journey took me across the world. I climbed Mt. Sinai alone in the dark, starting an hour and a half after more than 165 others and passing every single one of them on the way up, using the same alchemical breathwork, focus, and inner command I now teach. At the top, I shared communion and song as the sun rose with a church group that my guide had unknowingly placed me in the middle of. I became keenly aware that I was living a chapter of my own resurrection.

In Egypt, inside the **King's Chamber** of the Great Pyramid, I witnessed three undeniable physical miracles captured in photographs that confirmed what I had always known: the unseen is as real as anything we can touch. As my inner world transformed, my outer world did, too.

I became a **#1 Best Selling international author** of multiple books. I began speaking on stages across the globe, sharing space with icons like Jack Canfield, Mark Victor Hansen, Sharon Lechter, Les Brown, Marianne Williamson, and Marie Diamond. I was honored with a Doctorate of Divinity in recognition of my transformational work. I became a trusted speaker for Bill Walsh and Sir Dr. James Dentley, and stepped into roles as a teacher, mentor, and, eventually, an AI Consultant, helping others integrate intuitive intelligence and technology with soul. I was featured in documentaries and films that highlighted my abilities to read people at the deepest levels and catalyze real change.

Through it all, **my work crystallized**. I transformed my 90-day Rising Sovereign journey into a sacred, strategic container for high achievers, women and men who look successful on the outside but are quietly unraveling within. Inside that space, we don't chase hustle or performance. We build lives and businesses rooted in alignment, emotional mastery, and spiritual truth.

My rise became my method. My healing became my mastery.

Today, I teach my clients to:

- Identify and dissolve their repeating patterns.
- Break their internal contracts with suffering and scarcity.
- Awaken their Sensory Superpowers™ and trust their intuitive genius.
- Use the Breakthrough Code™ and Breakthrough Manifestation Code™ to create tangible, extraordinary results.

I've watched clients manifest **hundreds of thousands of dollars "out of nowhere,"** heal long-standing conditions, leave toxic environments, and step into visibility and leadership they once feared.

This isn't theory. **This work works.**

Through it all, I no longer see myself as the woman in the bathtub wondering if her life is over. I now celebrate that pivotal moment when I decided to be me and own it.

I am the woman who chose to stay. The woman who rose sovereign. The woman who became the fire.

Dream Life and Invitation to Join In

"I don't just want to live free. I want to lead others there, too."

Today, my life looks nothing like the day I sat in that bathtub.

I live with clarity and purpose. My business is a soul-aligned movement that spans continents. My clients are sovereign, successful, and deeply fulfilled.

I've paid off over $65,000 in debt. I've gone from making $55,000 a year to multiple six figures and beyond as a transformational guide, author, speaker, and mentor.

I've manifested international journeys, profound love, radiant health, and miracles that once felt like wishful thinking. But the greatest miracle is this: **I am finally me.** Unapologetically. Unshakably.

I don't chase. I attract. I don't prove. I embody. I don't rescue. I guide.

And I believe, with everything in me, that if you're reading this, your story has been preparing you, too.

Maybe you've been over-giving, over-achieving, or hiding the most powerful parts of yourself.

Maybe you've checked every box of external success, but still feel something is missing.

Maybe you've spent a lifetime surviving, but have never been shown how to rise.

If that's you, I see you. I know you because I was you. You don't need all the answers. You just need to know this: **Your story isn't over. In fact, the most powerful chapter may be the one you've yet to write.**

I built my **Rising Sovereign** framework for people like you, who are ready to stop running, start receiving, and step fully into the brilliance they've been dimming for years. The gifts I once denied are now the foundation of everything I do.

Using The Breakthrough Code™, the Breakthrough Manifestation Code™, and my Sensory Superpowers™ teachings, I help my clients dismantle their old patterns, awaken their intuitive genius, and create lives and businesses that feel like truth.

You may not be standing at the edge of a bathtub moment. But if you are reading these words, this is a pivotal moment.

You are more than what you've survived.

You are greater than you know.

You are loved in ways you cannot yet measure or fathom.

And I love you, too.

Are you ready to rise? Because I am here. And I am ready to walk with you.

Dr. Tammy De Mirza®

Dr. Tammy De Mirza®, internationally known as The Breakthrough Alchemist®, is a bestselling author, intuitive strategist, and transformational leader who has spent more than four decades guiding entrepreneurs, executives, and visionaries into their highest levels of personal power and prosperity. With her unparalleled ability to read the subconscious, interpret energetic patterns, and activate the five sensory superpowers, she helps high-achieving individuals break through the invisible barriers that keep them stuck, overwhelmed, or underperforming.

Her body of work includes the Breakthrough Manifestation Code™, Breakthrough Transformation Code™, Rising Sovereign Method™, and the 7-Figure Rising Sovereign Blueprint™, a proprietary system that empowers individuals to master emotional intelligence, collapse time, create aligned wealth, and embody sovereign leadership. Clients consistently experience profound and immediate shifts, clarity, breakthroughs in wealth and relationships, deep emotional integration, and rapid expansion in their businesses and lives.

Dr. Tammy's journey into sovereignty was forged through fire. After losing everything, including her home, financial stability, and sense of identity, due to a devastating betrayal, she rebuilt her entire life using the very principles she now teaches. Through intuitive alchemy and deep spiritual mastery, she paid off her debts, rebuilt her income by 434% in a single year, and rose into global influence, speaking around the world and transforming thousands of lives.

Today, she works with entrepreneurs, C-suite leaders, creators, and change-makers who are ready to rise beyond their limitations and lead from their higher selves. Her mission is simple and profound: to help people remember who they truly are, reclaim their intuitive genius, and build legacies rooted in sovereignty, purpose, and soul-aligned success.

Dr. Tammy De Mirza® stands as a living embodiment of what's possible when a person chooses their power, honors their gifts, and becomes the architect of their own destiny.

She recently spoke at the United Nations, where her work was formally recognized with multiple international honors, including a Lifetime Achievement Award, a Global Distinguished Leadership Award, and a Medal of Honor for exceptional leadership in global cooperation, conscious impact, and human empowerment. These awards were presented by Ambassador Dr. Hugues Sanon on behalf of COJEP, accredited to UNESCO and the European Parliament.

In New York, Tammy was also honored with a City Council Citation recognizing her as an Outstanding Citizen for building bridges of hope, justice, and sustainable peace across cultures and nations.

Ambassador Dr. Tammy De Mirza®
Tammy De Mirza, LLC
Greenville, South Carolina
864-430-8091
Tammy@TammyDeMirza.com
www.TammyDeMirza.com

Jeanett Modise

Redefining Success:
A High-Achiever's Path to Purpose & Freedom

The Breakdown Before the Breakthrough

The Morning My Body Said "Enough."

The Johannesburg sun streamed through the curtains of my hotel room, casting long shadows across the bed. It was one of those mornings that felt full of promise; bright skies, crisp air, and a keynote address I was excited to deliver. I had travelled in for a national coaching conference, and the day before, I was jogging outdoors, healthy, energized, and ready.

Then morning came. And everything changed.

I woke up, fully conscious, but something was wrong. Suddenly, I couldn't sit up. There was no pain at first, just stiffness. My upper body refused to respond. I tried again. Nothing. A strange, detached panic set in.

I rolled onto my side to maneuver upright, but the moment I stood, it hit me like a lightning strike; blinding, electric pain from my neck radiating down through my shoulder and left arm. My fingers tingled. I lost all sensation on the left side of my body. It hung onto my side, and I could barely walk.

The room spun. My breath caught. As a health professional, I knew the signs. And I feared the worst.

At the emergency room, I was rushed through a blur of IV analgesics, scans, x-rays, and neurological tests, and more. I remember the darkness of the X-ray room, the cold air, and the sterile silence. As the technician moved behind the machine, I stood still, tears silently streaking down my cheeks.

"Are you okay?" she asked gently. *"No,"* I whispered, *"but let's just do this."*

Hours later, a neurosurgeon stood at my hospital bed and delivered the verdict: Three cervical discs had slipped; C3, C4, and C5. The only solution was immediate surgery.

I wasn't just injured. I was immobilized. My body, once strong and dependable, had drawn a hard line. And in that moment, I understood: if I did nothing, I was going to lose far more than a speaking opportunity.

Behind the Success: A Storm Was Brewing

Long before the hospital bed and the neurosurgeon's ultimatum, I was a woman in motion. Constant motion. Driven, accomplished corporate executive and board director across various business sectors.

From the outside, my life was the very definition of success. I had built a multi-decade career leading people, culture, and business transformation at some of the world's most influential organizations, Hewlett-Packard, SAP, Sanlam, among others. I served as a trusted executive, shaping the futures of corporations, designing talent and culture strategies, and leading through complex change.

Beneath the surface, a quiet storm had been brewing. And deep down, I knew it.

There was a powerful awakening within me, a growing realization that I was heading toward a dangerous edge. My energy was strained, my soul was tired, and my health was slipping through the cracks of a schedule designed for performance, not preservation. I was managing people, strategy, boards, and even the national pandemic response, but I did not feature myself among these priorities.

It was a moment of truth. I knew something had to change.

That inner awakening only grew louder as I began engaging more deeply with senior leaders, especially women, across the business environment. I found that my story wasn't unique at all.

These women were brilliant, polished, and powerful. But behind the profiles and boardrooms, there was another reality: They were hustling, living in quiet burnout.

They were successful and high-performing, yet disconnected, exhausted, and emotionally depleted. They were operating on autopilot, constantly sacrificing themselves at the altar of corporate expectations. And the most heartbreaking part? Most of them thought it was normal. Even though companies offered wellness programs, flexible work arrangements, and health and well-being initiatives, very few women were able to leverage them in meaningful ways.

They were shackled by responsibility, work pressure, and self-imposed limitations, just as I had been.

The Calling I Couldn't Ignore

That's when my calling became unmistakably clear.

I was not meant to recover and move on. I was meant to rise and lean in, leveraging my experiences to guide other women before they hit the same wall I had. I was meant to proactively help them avoid the breakdown and define success in their own terms, without sacrificing their well-being, identity, or joy.

This calling wasn't born in a moment. It was the sum of every stage of my life, each one a challenge and a lesson.

From my early years as a professional nurse and midwife, where I learned the art of care and the power of human resilience…

For the years I spent juggling marriage, divorce, single motherhood, all together with full-time corporate executive jobs, and part-time studies, often with tears in my eyes and books at midnight…

To rise through the corporate career in complex, dynamic industries, managing huge budgets, global teams, large projects, and risk management, including leading the COVID pandemic…

Every phase taught me something essential. Every challenge gave me the insights I now tap into to add value to others.

Here's something important I want you to know:

When I felt that calling, I didn't walk away from my career. I didn't abandon everything I had built. I made a different choice, an aligned choice. I chose both.

I chose to continue my calling in corporate, serving people and organisations through executive leadership roles, and to pursue studies to become a certified business coach with a mission to add value and transform lives. Not either/or, both/and.

I believe women shouldn't have to choose between their personal and professional ambitions. Between leadership and well-being. Between legacy and a fulfilling life.

This mission became deeply personal: to help women break free from quiet burnout and build lives that are not only successful on paper but also fulfilling at the core.

Today, when I walk into coaching sessions with executives and entrepreneurs alike, I don't just bring credentials, I bring my lived experience. I know what it's like to run fast and smile big on an empty cup. I know what it's like to be a high performer while quietly longing for personal freedom. And I also know what it feels like to rise and thrive. That rising started the moment I said yes to myself.

Yes to my well-being.

Yes to my purpose.

Yes to my personal and financial freedom.

Yes to becoming a coach, a catalyst for personal and professional transformation and the guide I once needed.

The Moment I Chose Me

It was a quiet moment during an otherwise chaotic day. I had just wrapped another high-stakes board meeting, running on four hours of sleep and sheer willpower. The COVID-19 pandemic crisis just hit South Africa, and my instinct as a health professional took over. That, combined with my previous executive experience in leading facilities management, procurement, and people, I immediately assumed leadership of the pandemic management programme for our organisation across 35 countries, all while still recovering from major spinal surgery.

I remember staring at my reflection in the mirror that evening. I didn't recognize myself. My eyes were dim. My body was aching. My spirit was numb.

That's when the thought hit me: If I keep going like this, I'm going to disappear. Not physically, but piece by piece, my joy, my health, my peace, my purpose. Gone.

I heard myself say the words out loud: *"This is it. I want the Jeanett that I know back."*

That was the shift. I realized I had been surviving, not living. I knew if I didn't make a different choice, right then, I would lose more than just time. I would lose myself. And I wasn't willing to do that anymore.

From Recovery to Reinvention

What Moved Me Through the Pain…

Saying "yes" to myself wasn't a moment; it was a movement. A choice that echoed across every corner of my life.

After my health crisis and the deep personal awakening that followed, I didn't retreat. I didn't abandon the world I had spent decades building. I was working for an amazing organisation, and was offered to take as much time as I needed.

I chose both, not either /or. I chose to continue in my corporate leadership role doing what I love, and I chose to invest in my well-being and become the kind of coach I wished I had during my own quiet struggle. This guide understands both the weight of leadership and the necessity of holistic well-being.

That choice became my first step toward true transformation.

While still serving as an executive, I enrolled in a Master's program in Business Coaching. It was one of the few things that didn't feel like a burden; it felt like a breath of fresh air. Studying the craft of coaching became part of my own reflection, recovery, and transformation. Through the programme, I found pieces of myself I had neglected.

At first, I wondered if I could balance it all. The demands of my career didn't vanish. I was still leading teams, managing stakeholders, and showing up fully in high-stakes environments.

Something had shifted inside me.

I defined success in my own terms and actively invested in my well-being. I was no longer operating from emptiness; I was being fueled by purpose.

As I went through the programme, I also healed. I began guarding my mind, my energy, and my time more fiercely, saying no to what drained me, and yes to what aligned with my purpose and the new version of Jeanett I was becoming.

I integrated rest, nutrition, fitness, reflection, and further spiritual grounding into my life, not just as self-care, but as a strategy. I surrounded myself with mentors, accountability partners, and peers who could hold space for my dual path. And slowly, I began coaching others. Not just as a part of my leadership role and passion. As a calling.

Each session reminded me that everything I had walked through had prepared me for this moment, not just to survive it, but to overcome, rise, and arise. To lead others through it.

This wasn't a pivot. It was a homecoming.

The Rise: From the Valley to the Vision

Transformation is never linear… Once I chose to prioritize my well-being and align my life with a deeper purpose, I hoped the path ahead would be smoother. It wasn't. In many ways, the real work had only just begun.

Balancing my executive leadership role with this newfound calling wasn't easy. I successfully recovered from spinal surgery in half the time that the doctors had given me. I was still leading high-stakes board initiatives and maintaining my performance. And now, I was also becoming a professional coach and envisioning a completely new way to live and serve.

I had clarity, but I still had constraints.

At first, I did what I had always done: I relied on my resilience. I did research, studied, implemented, and integrated everything myself. I believed I could figure it out, especially because I was transitioning from a primary executive role to a portfolio career. I had the knowledge. I had experience. I had the capability and the desire to serve. I assumed that would be enough. But it wasn't.

I quickly realized I needed to reposition myself as a transformational coach, build a clear business model, develop systems, and learn how to package, price, and promote my services in a way that was sustainable and impactful.

I had the skill, but I didn't have the structure yet. And I waited too long to ask for help.

That's one of the mistakes I see high-achieving women make time and again. We're wired to take responsibility. To solve problems. To carry it all. But in business, and in life, clarity without support is a trap.

The more I tried to build alone, the harder it was to build momentum. I was giving away too much for free, hoping to "build exposure," but all over my demanding primary executive role. My life still revolved around work.

Even though my coaching was purpose-aligned, the systems I had built were still unsustainable.

Eventually, I started seeking support, not just from peers, but from successful global business coaches who had walked this path before me. They helped me shift my mindset, refine my message, and bring structure to my services.

They showed me how to stop trying to coach all leaders and start focusing on the women walking the path I had walked, who were sick and tired of being exhausted and ready for something more. That's when everything began to click. **I found my rhythm. My voice. My ideal client.**

I began coaching with greater confidence. My brand began to grow. I started designing offerings that were both transformational and profitable. I stopped undercharging and overdelivering. I got clear on how to market in a way that felt aligned, not forced.

Of course, there were still missteps. There were tech systems that added little value, and moments when I questioned everything.

However, each challenge became a learning experience, and a future teaching point I could incorporate into my coaching practice. I also learned that progress beats perfection. The truth is: I didn't walk through adversity for nothing.

I walked through for my own transformation. So I could help other women rise faster.

And now, I apply everything I've learned—*about mindset, systems, and soul-level alignment*—to help other women create the life and business they crave before burnout forces the decision for them.

Adversity taught me where the real work is. Now, I help others find their path, too.

The Freedom Formula: What Every Powerful Woman Needs to Rise

Reinvention isn't about becoming someone new; it's about reconnecting with who you were always meant to be.

That's what this journey gave me.

I became a woman who appreciates her worth and the value she brings. I've sustained my performance and remained grounded in my values. I lead from victory, and everything I do is aligned with my purpose. I didn't have to abandon my ambition; I just had to anchor it differently and be deliberate.

As a coach, I now partner with other powerful women to do the same, with clarity, conviction, and compassion.

Women who are tired of living on autopilot.

Women who are done with overgiving and underliving.

Women who are ready to redefine success and rise into the fullness of who they truly are.

With decades of experience in healthcare and leadership, I've created a coaching practice that supports these women in building fulfilling, integrated lives, where they no longer sacrifice their well-being for achievement.

Along the way, I've identified the core truths that helped me rise, truths I now call my Freedom Formula. They're not just tips. They're pillars that helped, and they're the foundation of everything I teach.

What Every Powerful Woman Needs to Rise

1. Your spirit is your source.

A strong spiritual foundation will keep you grounded and carry you when your strength runs out. It fuels peace, clarity, and perspective.

2. Your holistic well-being is non-negotiable.

Rest, nourishment, movement, and mindfulness aren't extras, they're essential to sustainable success and vibrant leadership.

3. **Your ecosystem shapes your outcomes.**

Build social connections and a support system that uplifts you, hold space for your growth, and protect your energy and purpose.

This is the foundation I stand on. And now, it's the same foundation I offer to every woman ready to rise.

From Pressure to Peace: My Freedom Formula

Dream Life and The Invitation to Rise…

Today, I live and lead from a place of alignment. I lead from victory.

I've built a coaching practice that enables me to do the work I was born to do, helping high-achieving women over 40 reclaim their lives before burnout chooses them. I now measure my value by how deeply I impact the women I serve, and how fully I honor the life God has given me.

I've traded long hours and constant pressure for strategic focus and a sense of spaciousness. I've cultivated diverse relationships that fuel me, not drain me. I have redefined what success means, not just in terms of personal and financial freedom, but also in terms of greater joy, peace, and purpose. I have built a business around my lifestyle and not the other way round. And best of all, I've discovered that transformation isn't about starting over.

It's about starting inward, and that progress beats perfection.

As you've read my story, I hope that something has stirred within you. A knowing. A whisper. A rising awareness that you've been running too hard for too long. That you've outgrown the life you're living. That you're ready for more, but not more pressure… more alignment, a fulfilling life with longevity.

If so, I want to say this clearly:

You don't have to keep doing it alone.

You don't have to wait for a breakdown to justify your breakthrough.

The life you yearn for, the business, the well-being, the freedom, is possible. I know, because I've lived on both sides at the same time.

Jeanett Modise

Executive Leader • Coach • Freedom Strategist

Jeanett Modise is an award-winning executive, certified business coach, and founder of The Freedom Business Accelerator™, a transformational program designed to help high-achieving women over 40 reclaim their energy, purpose, personal and financial freedom, before burnout chooses them.

With over 30 years of cross-industry experience in healthcare and executive leadership in the financial, technology, and mining sectors, including senior roles at global organizations like Hewlett Packard, SAP, and Sanlam, and multinational board experience. Jeanett is known for her bold executive presence, strategic insight, and heart-centered leadership.

But her most profound work began after a personal health crisis forced her to redefine success in her own terms. Now fully aligned with her purpose,

Jeanett empowers women to rise beyond quiet burnout and build fulfilling lives where well-being and ambition co-exist.

Her coaching combines deep spiritual grounding, real-world leadership experience, and actionable strategies to help women move from hustling to alignment, without sacrificing their performance, peace, or power. She helps women build lasting personal and financial freedom.

Jeanett is also a speaker, thought leader, and mentor committed to transforming how women lead, live, and rise, in corporate boardrooms and beyond.

Jeanett Modise
Johannesburg and Western Cape, South Africa
JeanettModise@gmail.com

The Business Accelerator:
Executive Freedom Checklist™

This assessment is designed for senior professional women in high-pressure corporate roles who want to build personal and financial independence through a purpose-driven business or portfolio career without burning out, starting over, or compromising their future.

https://FreedomAcceleratorco.com/LeadMagnet

Dr. Neja Zupan

Business Beyond Logic: The Energy Mastery System for Building Iconic Businesses

The Someday Syndrome: The Awakening

She lay still in my bed. I was only 25. My mother was gone.

I sat beside her, staring at the hands of a master cake artist, hands that had created beauty for countless couples but had never created the life she truly wanted. On her nightstand: a worn, unused ticket to Greece. Her dreams filed away for "after retirement," The mountain hut. The pastry shop. Travel. All waiting for "someday."

The truth screamed through me like lightning: **The real tragedy isn't that people die. The real tragedy is that people never truly live.**

Standing there, I realized I was becoming her.

Growing up, I was the sensitive one. Sensing storms before they arrived. By age six, the system labelled me "broken," defective.

My mother, brilliant but drowning in unexpressed grief, moved through our house like a ghost. Her dreams always filed away in the "someday" cabinet.

I learned early: **You sacrifice. You wait. You smile through the pain.**

I finished school. Built a career. Looked functional on the outside. Inside, I was suffocating. And **I saw the pattern everywhere** in my family.

My grandmother: cancer. My mother: cancer. My aunts, one by one: cancer.

Strong, capable women who could manage everything except their own dreams. They all sang the same sad song: *"Someday when I have time. When it's safe."*

When I looked at my own life, I saw their path ahead of me. The same sacrifice. The same waiting. The same dream deferred until it was too late. Unless I choose differently.

That morning, I made a decision: **I will not wait. Not for retirement. Not for the perfect moment. Not for someone else's permission.**

A fire was born inside me. A sacred commitment to break this cycle, to stop the epidemic of deferred dreams that convinces brilliant people to postpone their authentic lives until some mythical future that never arrives.

I started studying natural healing, began building my own business, and I learned to listen to the wisdom inside me rather than the rules outside me.

From that moment forward, my mission was clear: I would become a living example of what's possible when we choose alignment over waiting, energy over effort, frequency over fear. **The time was now. And I had to prove it was possible.**

The Blind Spot: When Good Intentions Aren't Enough

I meant what I said beside my mother's bed. The fire was real. The vow to break the cycle burned inside me with absolute clarity.

So I did what I thought was right. I left my regular job. I studied natural healing and spiritual modalities. I built my own business. I learned about energy work, ancestral patterns, and consciousness.

To everyone around me, it looked like I was finally living authentically. But there was a problem I couldn't see. **I was still betraying my soul.**

Despite all my external changes, the career pivot, the spiritual studies, the business, I was still trapped in the same survival patterns. Still suppressing emotions, still living by other people's rules, and still subordinating myself to everyone else's needs.

I was functioning from my mind, not my energy. From willpower, not alignment. From the same fractured foundation that had broken the women before me.

I told myself I was pursuing a purpose. But I was still abandoning myself. **I was chasing my dreams while betraying my soul.**

On the surface, I was doing everything "right." Building. Helping. Growing. But underneath, I was running the same operating system, the one that said my needs came last, the one that whispered I had to earn the right to happiness.

My body knew it.

In 2013, during meditation, something shifted. A voice. Clear. Undeniable. *"Neja... you have cancer."*

The doctors confirmed what my soul had already told me: aggressive breast cancer. Stage III+. BRCA gene positive. The same gene that had taken my grandmother. My mother. My aunts. I was on the same path.

Something inside me finally understood: This wasn't bad luck. This wasn't just genetics. This was my soul screaming loud enough that I finally had to listen. My body was forcing me to do what my mind had refused. That's when I understood the lie:

Transforming my mindset wasn't enough. I could change my thoughts, study spirituality, build a business, but if my energy remained fractured, nothing would shift.

I had spent years trying to fix an orchestra by rewriting the sheet music. I'd changed my thoughts, rewritten my beliefs, and reframed my story. But the musicians, my body, my nervous system, my cells, they were still out of tune. Still discordant. Still broken. **I didn't need a new mindset. I needed my entire being recalibrated.**

I had to tune every part of me back into harmony. **I had to become truly, deeply, radically aligned.**

The 5% Revolution: Choosing Impossible Odds Over Guaranteed Mediocrity

The consultation room felt like a boardroom where I was negotiating for my life. Three doctors sat across from me, their white coats like uniforms of authority. My sister sat beside me. We knew our family history too well.

The lead oncologist leaned forward, her voice grave, *"Without our complete protocol, surgery, ten cycles of three-day chemotherapy, thirty-five radiation sessions, five years of hormone therapy,* ***your survival rate is five percent."***

Five percent.

The silence stretched taut. My sister's breathing became shallow. The doctors waited for the inevitable breakdown, the desperate bargaining, the immediate surrender.

Instead, something else rose up: a clarity sharp as crystal and twice as unbreakable. I saw an opportunity and smiled with the genuine expression of someone who had just seen through the matrix.

"Doctor," I said, voice steady as bedrock, *"people play the lottery with odds of one in three hundred million. They mortgage their houses for chances so slim they'd need a microscope to see them."*

I sat back, feeling power flow through me like electricity finding its conductor. *"You're offering me five percent. Why would I refuse odds that are infinitely better than what people willingly gamble with every day?"*

The youngest doctor shifted uncomfortably. *"Ms. Zupan, I don't think you understand the gravity…"*

"Thank you. I understand." The words came from depths older than fear. *"But let me ask you something. Among the five of us here, who is immortal?"*

Pin-drop silence.

"All of us will die eventually. The only question is: will we die having lived, or will we die having waited, scared, unfulfilled?"

I knew insanity was doing the same thing over and over and expecting different results. **I refused to repeat my family's pattern.**

I thought of my mother's worn Greece ticket. Every woman in my family who had followed the prescribed path, be responsible, be realistic, be safe, and carried their songs to the grave, unsung.

"I have five percent," I said, standing with the dignity of a queen. *"I want to let you know, I already bought the ticket."*

"What ticket?" the lead oncologist asked.

"Ticket for the grand lottery prize," I answered. ***"The ticket to my authentic life. The one my mother never used. The one every woman in my family let expire in their hands."***

I continued, *"You're all already invited to my hundredth birthday celebration."* I knew I had crossed a threshold with no return. This wasn't reckless abandon. **This was a conscious choice.** This wasn't denial. **This was deeper knowing.**

I wasn't going to fight cancer. I was going to recalibrate the frequency that had made space for it. That moment wasn't just a medical decision. It was a spiritual and energetic transformation, the doorway to everything I was born to become.

Frequency Over Force: Awakening Multidimensional Intelligence in Business

I turned inward. I chose to see cancer not as my enemy, but as my greatest teacher, a wake-up call to show me what needed to change. My intention wasn't to kill the cancer. It was to restore what had been buried inside me: my true self. And then I started the actual work.

I learned to calm my nervous system, the part of me in survival mode my whole life. I detoxified my body, releasing old trauma and grief stored in my cells. I worked with my body's natural intelligence. I leaned into spiritual technologies, not from a textbook, but by listening to the divine codes within me.

I stopped outsourcing my intuition and started trusting what I knew. I didn't just recover. I optimized.

In six months, I was declared cancer-free. But the real miracle wasn't the diagnosis. It was who I became. I emerged realigned, re-encoded, and reawakened. And that's when I truly understood: **Real change doesn't come from forcing yourself. It comes from aligning your energy with who you really are.**

When I came back to the business world with this new awareness, everything looked different.

I understood how a liver detox protocol could shift someone's capacity for financial abundance. When the liver releases stored anger and resentment, it creates space for receiving prosperity. I could perceive how unresolved grief manifested as self-sabotage in business launches, the heart protecting itself from rejection by unconsciously creating failure. I witnessed how ancestral patterns of scarcity showed up in pricing strategies and visibility fears, generations of "don't stand out" programming running through the nervous system.

These weren't mind problems. These were energy problems.

When I started applying this understanding to my business, the shift was exponential. I could feel which offers were aligned and which were draining. I could sense which collaborations were frequency matches.

Instead of running on mental willpower, I began operating from energetic coherence. The results? Flow. Clarity. Potent offers. Sustainable revenue. Real impact.

By contemplating the changes in my life, I came to a realization… Throughout my journey, I have worked with many incredible teachers. A detox expert. Energy healers. A mindset coach. Business coaches. Each was brilliant. But each worked in their own lane.

They were all right. Just the knowledge and wisdom were separated. And I had spent years treating myself like separate parts.

No one was showing me how my childhood wounds lived in my blood and organs, how my suppressed emotions created blockages in my energy field, how those blockages influenced my business decisions. No one explained how my ancestral scarcity patterns showed up as underpricing, how my fear of visibility was stored in my nervous system, how my mother's unfulfilled dreams were running my unconscious sabotage patterns, how my childhood abandonment wounds affected my ability to set boundaries with clients.

I worked on my thoughts separately. My emotions separately. My body separately. My spirit separately. But what if you're not separate parts? What if everything is interconnected?

That's when I discovered that my success was based on a simple truth: I had connected 4 parts of the human as a whole being. This is what **I now call multidimensional intelligence**, the connection between all layers of human being:

1. **Mental Intelligence:** your thoughts, beliefs, mind (IQ)
2. **Emotional Intelligence:** your heart, feelings (EQ)
3. **Somatic Intelligence:** your body, stored memories (neuroscience)
4. **Spiritual Intelligence:** your ability to perceive and conduct energy and use intuition (SQ)

Most people know about these intelligences. Therapists work with emotional intelligence. Neuroscientists understand somatic intelligence. A mindset coach focuses on changing your beliefs. Business coaches focus on mental intelligence. Spiritual teachers activate spiritual intelligence.

But here's what I discovered: Most people work on one. Maybe two. **Transformation requires integrating all four as one unified system: Your mental, emotional, somatic, and spiritual intelligence all point toward the same goal. THEN your business becomes magnetic. Clients show up. Pricing flows. Launches succeed.**

That's what I became obsessed with exploring: How to integrate BOTH the energy AND the business? What if you could be spiritually aligned AND financially successful? How to build a thriving business AND stay peaceful in a healthy body?

Those questions led me to synthesize what had been separated.

5 key points when transformation occurs:

1. When you shift the energy in your body and nervous system, your business transforms. It's not about forcing success. It's about aligning what's inside with what you're building outside.
2. When your body releases stored resentment, abundance flows. You're no longer fighting scarcity at a cellular level.
3. When your heart feels safe and protected, launches succeed. You're no longer sabotaging yourself from fear of rejection.
4. When your spiritual intelligence is aligned with your goals, you perceive opportunities you couldn't see before. Your intuition becomes your compass.
5. When your mental intelligence, somatic intelligence, emotional intelligence, and spiritual intelligence are working together, that's when everything changes.

That's multidimensional intelligence in action. And when you master that? Everything transforms.

The Dragon Laws: Multidimensional Intelligence in Practice

As I mastered multidimensional intelligence, I discovered something:

transformation isn't just a concept. It's lived. It's practical. It shows up as three core principles that guide every decision, every leadership move, every moment of alignment.

From that multidimensional intelligence awakening, three principles emerged. Three Dragon Laws. They show you how to activate and live it.

As I applied these laws to my business and life, everything shifted.

Before: I made decisions from anxiety. I checked my email fifty times a day. I said yes to every client. I undercharged. I stayed small and felt empty.

After: I made decisions from a calm place. I check my email twice a day. I said no to misaligned clients. I charged what I was worth. I claimed space in the market.

And people noticed.

They wanted to know how I was making decisions with such clarity, how I stayed aligned even when facing challenges, and how my business could flow rather than be forced. So, I began teaching what I had discovered. These three Dragon Laws became the foundation of everything I would share.

1. **Think Beyond What You're Told: Trust Your Deep Knowing**

Challenge conventional systems that disconnect you from your power. Listen to your energetic intelligence even when it contradicts logic.

What this means in practice: Instead of following your industry's "best practices," test what works for YOUR nervous system. If a business tactic makes you anxious, it's misaligned, even if it's "proven."

2. **Peace Is the Portal**

Anchor major decisions from your highest signal, not urgency. Regulate your nervous system as a leadership practice.

What this means in practice: When you feel urgency pushing you to decide, pause. Get calm first. Decide from that place of peace. You'll make 80% better choices.

3. Challenges Are Invitations

See every breakdown as a frequency upgrade in disguise. Extract wisdom from pain and stagnation.

What this means in practice: When something breaks down, don't ask *"What went wrong?"* Ask *"What is this teaching me?"* Your challenges become your credentials.

You might be wondering: What if I get this wrong?

Your body won't lie to you. If a business opportunity makes your chest tight, it's misaligned, even if it looks good on paper. The tightness, the dread, the heaviness, that's your frequency telling you this isn't aligned.

How is this different from other frameworks?

Most business frameworks ignore your body completely. They say, *"Work harder, think better, optimize faster."*

The Dragon Laws are the reverse.

We say: Get aligned first, then strategy flows. Recalibrate your frequency before you optimize your tactics. Your body is smarter than any strategy.

These three principles work for anyone ready to lead authentically. They are not formulas. The Dragon Laws are energetic blueprints. Because the world doesn't need more strategy, it needs more authentic leaders who create from truth, not trauma. This is how we change business from the frequency up, and this is exactly what happened when I began teaching the Dragon Laws.

People applied them. Their businesses transformed. Their lives became magnetic. Their peace deepened. Their impact multiplied. They didn't just survive. They flourished.

That's when I realized: **The Dragon Laws were about one thing, reclaiming your own authority, your own truth, your own throne.**

The moment you're ready to activate these laws is the moment everything changes. The question is: Which law will you claim first?

Your business is waiting for this. Your life is ready for this. Your body knows it's time. YES!

Business Beyond Logic: What Becomes Possible When You Claim Your Throne and Live The Dragon Laws

When you activate the three Dragon Laws, everything transforms.

Law 1: Think Beyond What You're Told

My clients stop following "best practices" that drain them. They test what works for THEIR nervous system. They say no to proven tactics that feel wrong. Their anxiety drops. Their authority rises.

This is where **Scaling Business in Resonance** begins, learning to scale from alignment, not force. From your frequency, not from industry formulas.

Law 2: Peace Is the Portal

They stop making decisions due to urgency. They pause. They get calm. They decide from peace. Suddenly, 80% better choices. Launches that flow. Pricing that feels aligned.

This is exactly what the **Guided Audio Meditation: Peace is the Portal** teaches you, how to anchor in peace so every decision becomes magnetic. Not someday. Every single day.

Law 3: Challenges Are Invitations

Every breakdown becomes a breakthrough. Every stagnation becomes wisdom. They stop asking *"What went wrong?"* and start asking *"What is this teaching me?"* Their challenges become their credentials. Their struggles become their strength.

This is the foundation of the MasterClass Series: Unlocking Inner Mastery through Multidimensional Intelligence Awakening, a deep dive with leaders and change-makers who are ready to extract the wisdom from everything and lead at a legacy level.

When you live all three Dragon Laws, when you think beyond what you're told, anchor in peace, and extract wisdom from challenges, you activate multidimensional intelligence as your operating system. **You don't just survive. You become magnetic.**

But this work isn't for everyone.

It's for leaders ready to stop performing and start leading from truth. For change-makers ready to scale with integrity. For visionaries ready to build from the inside out.

Maybe you've achieved success, but it feels empty. Maybe you're stuck in a life that looks good but doesn't fit your frequency. Maybe you've always known you were here to lead, but haven't known how to unlock that.

If that's you, it's not a coincidence. It's a calling.

Here's how to begin:

Start with Peace is the Portal: the guided audio meditation that anchors you in calm decision-making. This is foundational. Do this first.

Then scale with Scaling Business in Resonance: learn to build a business that flows instead of forces, that honours your frequency while multiplying your impact.

Go deeper with the Unlocking Inner Mastery, MasterClass Series: for leaders and change-makers ready to fully awaken multidimensional intelligence and lead at a frequency that changes everything.

Most leaders feel the shift within weeks. All of them report the same thing: Everything changes when you claim the Dragon Laws.

Which Dragon Law are you ready to claim first?

Your time is now. Choose your entry point.

Because the world needs what you're here to create.

Dr. Neja Zupan

Dr. Neja Zupan is a Global Energy Master and founder of Energy Masters Academy, with over three decades of experience guiding change-makers to understand that inner energy, not strategy, determines whether they lead from pressure or presence.

She guides change-makers to master their inner energy, so they attract more opportunities with less effort, embody greater vitality, and become increasingly magnetic to their ideal customers. When you elevate your inner energy, outer achievements naturally follow.

Using practical, body-based techniques rooted in nervous system recalibration and emotional clearing, she helps leaders release hidden stress patterns: physical tension, inherited emotional pressure, and unprocessed fatigue so that they can operate from calm strength, not force. When you're energetically aligned, your impact becomes an expression of who you are. This is Business Beyond Logic, where decisions emerge from wholeness, not resistance.

Through The Ultimate Energy Empowerment System, Scaling Business in Resonance, Unlocking Inner Mastery through Multidimensional Intelligence Awakening, and the Mastering Energy Academy, she empowers leaders to master their energy and create sustainable impact.

Her work is grounded in profound lived truth. Diagnosed with aggressive Stage III+ cancer carrying the BRCA gene, the same genetic marker that had taken her grandmother, mother, and aunts. Dr. Neja recalibrated her entire being through energy work. In six months, she was cancer-free. More importantly, she was reborn. That experience revealed the fundamental truth driving all her work: transformation comes through alignment, not force. She embodies what she teaches.

Those who work with her don't just perform better; they become more fully themselves, operating from a completely different source. They lead from inner authority, make decisions that feel congruent, and create impact that sustains from their authentic power.

Dr. Neja Zupan
Dr. Neja Zupan Institute
Info@NejaZupan.com
www.LinkedIn.com/in/DrNejaZupan
www.Instagram.com/Dr.Neja.Zupan.Institute
www.Facebook.com/DrNejaZupanInstitute
www.TikTok.com/@Dr_Neja_Zupan_Institute
www.YouTube.com/@DrNejaZupanInstitute

The Dragon Laws: Your Business Beyond Logic Toolkit

What becomes possible when you claim your throne and live the Dragon Laws

When you activate the three Dragon Laws, everything transforms.

When you live all three Dragon Laws, when you think beyond what you're told, anchor in peace, and extract wisdom from challenges, you activate multidimensional intelligence as your operating system.

You don't just survive. You become magnetic. But this work isn't for everyone.

It's for leaders ready to stop performing and start leading from truth. For change-makers ready to scale with integrity. For visionaries ready to build from the inside out.

Maybe you've achieved success, but it feels empty. Maybe you're stuck in a life that looks good but doesn't fit your frequency. Maybe you've always known you were here to lead but haven't known how to unlock that.

If that's you, it's not a coincidence. It's a calling.

Your time is now. Choose your entry point.

Because the world needs what you're here to create.

www.NejaZupan.com/Business-Beyond-Logic-Resources/

Brenda Vega

The Mantle and the Marketplace: Where Spiritual Authority Meets Wealth Without Compromise

Commands and Demands

I could feel my heart pounding in my chest as I sat in front of my laptop, staring into the quiet glow of the Zoom screen, adjusting my lighting, sipping coffee that had gone lukewarm, and preparing to deliver what was supposed to be a polished, professional business talk. It was a cold December morning in 2024, and hundreds of women were gathering on the other side of the screen. Entrepreneurs, leaders, seekers of "the next level." They were waiting. They were watching.

I had done this before. Speaking has never intimidated me. As a pastor, an apostle in my church, I'd preached sermons, taught classes, led retreats, and carried rooms for decades, but **this felt different.**

The well-known coach who invited me to speak at her annual event was giving me an opportunity to stop playing small and expand my boundaries. I had the script. I had prepared. I knew exactly how this was supposed to go.

But something in my spirit wouldn't settle.

There was a weight on my chest, not fear, but *tension.* The kind that comes when you know you're standing on the edge of something new that may cost you your comfort. When the line between safety and surrender stretches tighter than it ever has before. And then, I heard Him… ***"Bless Them."***

Just two words. No explanation. No safety net. But I knew exactly what He meant.

In that moment, I faced a choice every "called" woman eventually faces: **Do I perform… or do I obey?** I tossed the script aside. I took a steadying breath, and the words came rushing out.

"God did not anoint you for survival. He wants you to be rich!"

There. I said it. Out loud. On a business stage. To a business audience and some raised-eyebrow Believers.

I could feel the atmosphere shift even through the screen. I taught a little for context, but then shifted. I began to decree and declare truths I had tucked away inside church walls for far too long.

I spoke of life instead of strategy alone. I blessed their hands, their minds, their money, and their callings. I reminded them that they were fearfully and wonderfully made, that the blessing of the Lord makes rich and adds no sorrow. I called them into divine alignment. I called forth the hidden treasures and released an anointing over every woman listening.

By the time I finished, the chat was exploding, and emails poured in. Within hours, more than a hundred women had requested my gift, and new clients were reaching out. I was thrilled!

The real miracle wasn't in the numbers. Something exploded in me. The old box shattered. The voice that told me I had to choose between God and business went silent.

That morning, I stopped hiding and started rising. I would never again separate my spiritual mantle of authority from my wealth mission.

From the Pulpit to the Platform

Long before business stages and Zoom rooms, there was a classroom and a pulpit.

For most of my adult life, I was a teacher, a mother, an adventurous soul of unshakeable faith. I spent fifteen years teaching school in North Carolina, faithfully raising my three daughters while my then-husband served in the Marine Corps. I always had a small business on the side: a skin care consultant, a home products distributor, and a Christmas decor crafter.

My life looked wonderful.

Behind closed doors, I was navigating the growing distance between two people who no longer shared the same vision. Futures are no longer aligned. Tensions escalated. Clear lines had to be drawn as incidents of violence occurred.

When that relationship ended, I didn't unravel; **I rebuilt.**

Although there were times I felt alone and my faith was challenged, God was never far. He was not absent during the breaking. He was preparing me for the making.

Years later, I remarried, this time to a man whose devotion to God matched my own. Together, we were ordained as pastors, and teaching the Word of God became a natural extension of who I already was.

Bible studies filled our home every Thursday night. Women gathered. Laughter and tears flowed. Deep friendships were built. Healing happened. Transformation followed.

The pulpit became my home base. I poured myself into every soul who walked through our doors. Over the years, I ministered across the country and overseas, planted churches internationally, and was elevated to the office of the apostle.

Fulfilled, and yet, I felt a holy tension. A whisper. ***"There's more."***

Not more titles.

Not more applause.

More reach.

More impact.

More assignments beyond the four walls.

And that whisper terrified me. But **I listened. I learned. I obeyed.**

This was before everything lived online. So, I invested in business coaching. I explored how to take my voice beyond church walls and into the global marketplace. I studied online communication and entrepreneurship, not to replace my calling, but to expand it.

I was not leaving the ministry. I was translating God's wealth principles to the business world.

I remember my first coach clearly. She was polished, successful, and exactly who I thought I needed. I had poured my heart into building an online program for Christian women that integrated business strategy with biblical truth. I was excited to share it with her.

She glanced at it for two seconds. *"Too spiritual,"* she said. *"You can't sell God. No one wants to buy that. This is business."* She said it as if I had tracked mud across her white carpet!

I admit, I was rattled. What was she talking about? I "sold" Jesus every time I stepped into a pulpit, often to people who did not yet know they needed salvation.

So, I tried again. Coach after coach. Course after course. I kept getting some version of the same thing:

"Keep ministry and business separate."

"You'll need to tone that down to be marketable."

"Faith is personal and unprofessional in the business setting."

They offered cookie-cutter business plans, templated messaging, and clever marketing hacks. They suggested I become a parenting coach, a divorce coach, anything palatable and "safe." I softened my language. Diluted my message. I tried to make myself more "universal." More acceptable. And every time I did, something in me fractured.

None of it made room for who I really was. None of it honored the God I serve or the mantle I carry.

Soon, I realized that in chasing the approval of coaches who didn't recognize the power of my message, I had drifted from my assignment. I was no longer building the Kingdom blueprint God had for me.

They wanted me safe. God wanted me to surrender. Then the world shut down.

The Line in the Sand

COVID forced everything online. Churches and businesses closed. Websites were booming. Facebook became the dominant social media platform. Ministry went digital overnight. Technology was not my native language. The online world felt like a foreign country I had no passport for! Suddenly, I had no choice but to figure it out. I learned how to use Zoom. I learned how to livestream and navigate new tech tools just to keep the ministry alive. It was exhausting, but it was also an opportunity.

God was still whispering, ***"There's more."*** And in the middle of all that disruption, clarity came.

I knew there were other faith-filled women out there just like me whom God was calling into business. I saw brilliant, God-fearing women everywhere—*leaders, coaches, teachers, pastors' wives*—who were anointed to impact lives but terrified to sell online, undercharging for their gifts, shrinking in rooms that needed their voice. Women called by God to make bold moves in business. Women tired of trying to fit their round, anointed selves into a square, secular business mold. Women who were craving a place to be mentored, equipped, and commissioned without having to leave their faith at the door.

Women who wanted purpose over performance. Prosperity without apology. Women who needed someone to hold space for their voice until they were strong enough to speak out for themselves.

That's when the Divine Woman Unleashed was born in my heart. That's when my true assignment clicked into place. I don't just teach women how to build a business; I help them identify their anointing and wear their mantle boldly, just like Elisha did in 2 Kings 2.

Obedience in Action

Now that I had my identity straight, I was determined to build God's version of success, not everyone else's.

But I had to figure out the thing keeping me invisible online. I was comfortable in rooms of hundreds of real people, but shy on camera in front of potentially unseen millions of faces! What would they say? How would they judge me? *Really, Apostle Brenda?* Yep. But I knew if I kept shrinking, I'd never fulfill my assignment. And worse, I'd be modeling that same fear for the women I was meant to lead!

The first step was reclaiming my voice. Spiritually and strategically.

I stopped filtering my message. I stopped playing it safe. I allowed myself to show up fully, faith, fire, and all.

I revisited my systems and rebuilt with intentionality. My offers. My messaging. My presence.

Through spirit-led discernment, I found a few mentors who "got me." Amazing businesswomen like Alexis Caldicott and Buki Ekeowa, just to name two, who gave me a glimpse of what my business could look like and modeled for me how to lead boldly with my faith in online spaces.

I began appearing on virtual events and summits where women were invited into unapologetic conversations about faith and business. Each event proved that there is a remnant of women craving more of God's spirit in every area of their lives, including their business. They are not looking for another blueprint. They are looking for a breakthrough.

Journey Through the Weeds

Second, I wish I could tell you that the moment I chose to obey the Holy Spirit and take His message to the marketplace, everything fell into place immediately. It didn't.

Yes, clarity came. Yes, the weight of holding back lifted. But clarity didn't pay bills. And obedience didn't cancel obstacles. If anything, when you are **in the process of becoming**, the road gets harder before it gets holy.

Yes, I made the brave decision to walk in my full truth, reclaim my voice, but I realized I had no roadmap. I still fumbled through sales pages and funnel software. Trying to piece together what every coach had told me, launch a course, start a podcast, and coach one-on-one until I "found my lane."

Yes, I tried it all. Spent money I didn't really have. Bought programs I didn't really need. Hired coaches I shouldn't have. Burnt myself out, wanted to quit, and sometimes felt like retreating to my pulpit.

Some days my head was spinning!

I built landing pages that got zero opt-ins, launched offers that got crickets. I cried in frustration more times than I can count, wondering if I'd made a mistake. Wondering if I'd misunderstood what God told me. Wondering if obedience had a return policy.

I remember one night, sitting in front of my laptop, staring at a Canva document I'd been trying to create for hours. My shoulders were tense. My spirit was weary. And I whispered, *"Lord, I'm doing everything you said... but it's still not working."*

And that's when I heard Him again. ***"Because you're still building their system, not mine."***

That cut deep. Because it was true. I had removed the filters from my message, but I hadn't removed them from my method. I was still chasing strategies instead of stewarding the assignment.

So, I slowed down. I stopped looking for the next shiny formula. I asked myself, what do I already know works? And the answer was clear:

Community.

Voice.

Anointing.

Obedience.

So, I planned and hosted a retreat for a group of Kingdom women. I needed that weekend as much as they did. Ironically, I called it **Transformed Under Pressure,** a space to talk openly about money, faith, identity, and legacy. I didn't try to sell anything. I just poured into them. Prophesied over them. Spoke life into their lives, their dreams, their businesses.

And something miraculous happened. **They left transformed.** Weeks later, emails kept coming.

"You helped me believe again."

"I raised my prices and signed two clients."

"My mindset and money shifted."

That retreat didn't make me rich. But it made me certain. **This was part of the model.**

After that, I understood how I didn't need to try to scale someone else's system and started building what I call a *Kingdom enterprise*, a business rooted in spiritual truth, aligned with divine identity, and driven by real transformation.

Now, let me be honest… even after that amazing, satisfying experience, I still made mistakes. I undercharged. I over-delivered. I said yes when I should've said no. I tried to run Facebook ads before my offer was ready. I built an email list but didn't know how to nurture it.

But every misstep was a tuition payment in the School of Becoming.

And those failures? They were all a part of the process. They made me the mentor I am today. Because I've walked through the weeds, I know what it's like to hear the "call" but not have the map. I know what it's like to pray for a breakthrough while duct-taping a funnel together at midnight. I know the sting of silence after launching your "best idea yet." I know the loneliness of being too spiritual for the business world and too ambitious for the church world. And I know the cost of trying to figure it all out alone.

That's why I created a different path for the women I serve. A space where you don't have to mute your faith or water down your power. A space where you are **mentored, seen, equipped, and activated** to build a business that is not just about money, but a Kingdom tool to enrich yourself and all the others that are waiting to follow you, while advancing God's kingdom on earth.

Dragon Strategies

Walking through the weeds didn't just test my faith; **it refined my fire.**

I didn't come out the same woman who walked in. I came out **sharpened. Strengthened. Anointed for the assignment.**

I became more than a messenger; I became a mentor, not just in the spirit, but in strategy. I learned how to architect programs that move people. I learned to sell high-ticket offers with heart and conviction. I developed a prophetic voice in the business space, something I had known was necessary to model.

I also got smarter. I stopped chasing validation and learned to trust my discernment. I built out real systems to support my message and my peace. I integrated strategy with anointing. I learned to lead from overflow, not obligation. And most importantly, I stopped playing small in rooms I was meant to own.

This journey wasn't about building a business. It was about becoming the kind of leader I wish I'd had when I was lost in the wilderness of strategy and self-doubt.

So now, I equip women like I once was.I tell them these three basic truths.

Three Unshakable Truths for the Called Entrepreneur

1. Listen to the Holy Spirit

Your first business partner is God. If you can't hear His voice, you'll follow too many others. *"My sheep know my voice,"* so tune out the noise and lean into divine direction. Schedule a weekly business meeting with God. Bring an agenda. Learn to listen! Prioritize your meeting with Him. Make Him the real CEO of your business.

2. God's Plan Is Prosperity, Not Poverty

Jeremiah 29:11 and John 10:10 weren't written just to inspire you; they were written to equip you. Stop apologizing for wanting wealth. Your abundance may be someone else's roadmap. Remember, though, it's not about the money for money's sake. It's about the mission.

3. Find a Container That Honors Your Calling

Proverbs 27:17, Ecclesiastes 4:9-12. You were never meant to build alone. Find a mentor who recognizes your anointing and empowers you to carry it with boldness. Safe spaces build strong leaders.

This is how I slay dragons now, and this is how I teach other women to slay theirs.

The Assignment I Carry Now

Today, I live a life I once only imagined. I stand as a Marketplace Apostle and live a life where my voice is no longer filtered, where my message is no longer restrained, and where my faith fuels every part of my life, including my business. But the real reward is not the income or success of the programs.

For me, the joy comes from watching women step into their divine identity, come alive, and shine from the inside out. It's witnessing them become the Divine Women Unleashed on the world!

I have watched them trade confusion for clarity.

Fear for faith. Hustle for holy alignment.

I have watched women who once whispered begin to speak with authority. Women who were once undercharged begin to own their value. Women who once shrank in rooms begin to lead them.

I know there are more of you.

You are the woman behind the screen, wondering if your message is too spiritual for business… or too bold for your circle.

You have invested in courses and followed the templates. Tried the formulas. Softened your voice. Adjusted your language and dimmed your fire And still, something feels off. Because you were never created to fit into someone else's framework.

You were created to carry something precious, **a vessel of purpose created by God.**

You have been praying for confirmation of your cry, *"God, there has to be more."*

Let this be it.

God did not plant that dream in you to frustrate you. He planted it because there are people attached to your obedience. The world needs what's inside of you. That idea, that message, that movement, it's not random. **It's a revelation.** There is an impact attached to your voice. There is wealth attached to your alignment, and you do not have to walk it out alone.

What I have built is not a coaching program. I've built a divine container.

A place where Kingdom women are mentored, refined, and released.

A place where your mantle and your marketplace finally meet.

A place where you stop apologizing for your anointing and start building with it.

Your mantle is tied to your mission.

The marketplace is not hostile territory.

It is mission ground.

The question is no longer whether you are called.

The question is whether you are ready to rise.

The mantle is in front of you.

Pick it up and try it on.

By the way, those coaches who said I couldn't sell faith and business, guess who their target audiences are today!

Brenda Vega

Brenda Vega is a Marketplace Apostle, spiritual midwife, and catalyst for Kingdom-driven women entrepreneurs who refuse to choose between their calling and their cash flow. Known affectionately as "Apostle B," Brenda is an internationally recognized Faith and Business Mentor, Apostolic leader, and creator of The Mantle Maker Mastermind™, a transformative framework equipping women to build profitable, Spirit-led businesses rooted in purpose, power, and biblical prosperity principles. She is the founder of The Divine Woman Unleashed and Women Empowered by the Word communities.

For more than two decades, Brenda has served as a pastor, apostolic mentor, ministry founder, educator, and entrepreneur, growing churches, healing hearts, and raising leaders across the United States, Brazil, and international locations.

A former Department of Defense educator and Executive Director of a Domestic Violence Agency, she has mentored hundreds of women through life-changing Bible studies, retreats, and ministry programs.

As a longtime entrepreneur, from building a successful skincare business to representing military wives at Pentagon working groups, Brenda understands firsthand the courage, faith, and resilience required to walk out a God-given calling while navigating real-life challenges.

She now brings that same transformative authority into the business world. She doesn't just teach strategy; she activates destiny. She doesn't just coach; she imparts.

Her mission is clear: to raise a generation of women who are in divine alignment with their divine assignment, who refuse to shrink in the face of adversity, and who boldly take their place as CEOs, visionaries, and world changers.

She's known for her elegance and authority, her ability to speak truth with grace, and her unwavering commitment to raising women who will transform economies and advance the Kingdom, one anointed business at a time.

Brenda is Mom to three adult daughters and Nana to two granddaughters. She loves strolling along the beach, reading voraciously, enjoying musicals like Hamilton and The Greatest Showman, and her latest hobby, birdwatching!

Brenda Vega
Brenda Vega Coaching Solutions
Jacksonville, North Carolina
BrendaVegaSpeaks@gmail.com
www.BrendaVegaCoachingSolutions.com
www.Facebook.com/BrendaVega802211
www.LinkedIn.com/in/BrendaVegaSpeaks
Instagram: BrendaVegaSpeak

COMMAND YOUR DAY!
Seven Days Of Devotions To Ignite Your Entrepreneurial Spirit

Command Your Day! is a spirit-led AUDIO and JOURNALING DEVOTIONAL designed for faith-driven women who know they are called for more, but want more clarity, courage, and alignment to move forward.

Over seven days, you'll be guided to quiet the noise, hear God's voice with greater confidence, and realign your mornings with Heaven's strategy for your life and business. Each day includes prophetic insights, scripture, guided reflection, and powerful declarations to help you overcome fear, break hesitation, and take bold, faith-filled action.

This is not just a devotional, it's an activation.

https://bit.ly/3Ol8mEj

Marina Tudor

Dragon Queens Lineage: One Woman's Mission to Reclaim the Gen X Feminine Power

The Night I Almost Died

I didn't want to go to the hospital. Not two months earlier. Not two weeks earlier. Not that day.

I had been telling everyone I was fine, that the exhaustion, the shortness of breath, the pain, it was manageable. I knew my body. I knew how to heal. I wasn't afraid. But the truth was, **I couldn't even speak without gasping for air**. My lungs were shutting down, but my consciousness, or maybe my pride, kept saying, *"I've got this."*

But my brother *knew*.

Sebastian is four years younger than me, and the one human being on this planet I've always felt cosmically tethered to. He lives in Germany, and we don't speak every day, but when we do, there's a frequency between us, a knowing. That day, when he called, I couldn't even speak. My voice collapsed under the weight of no oxygen.

And he ***knew.***

His instincts kicked in like a siren. He started looking for flights, trying to get to the U.S. But quickly realized he wouldn't make it in time. Or worse… I wouldn't.

So he called our family here in the States. And he yelled. Not from anger, but from a deep, protective, soul-level panic. ***"Get her to the hospital. Now."***

My mother, a doctor herself, had been trying to get me to go for weeks. My partner, Doug, had pleaded with me, tears in his eyes. Earlier that day, my mom and my aunt drove from Virginia to Maryland. Doug was waiting. And when they arrived at my house, I saw it all on their faces, the fear, the urgency, the love.

Finally, I said yes.

That night in the hospital, I learned just how close to death I had been. It was late, my second night in the ICU. My lungs were collapsing. My oxygen was almost nonexistent. My body was riddled with clots. Doctors told me later I had days left, maybe hours. But that night, I didn't need them to tell me. My soul knew.

What I didn't know was how loud love could be.

I reached for my phone with trembling hands, fevered fingers barely able to type. My only thought was of my brother, my baby brother in Germany. A surgeon. A husband. A father. He had no idea what was happening in my body in those moments.

I started to write him a message:

"I'm dying. It's okay, I'm not afraid. I'll be around. I love you."

Something stopped me. Not fear... Not hesitation... **Spirit.**

I tried again and again. **300 times.** The words came. But I couldn't hit send. It was as if Spirit itself kept tapping my hand away. As if love had hands.

So I just kept writing. *"I love you. I'll still be here."*

My body was shutting down. But my soul wasn't finished. I focused on him, my love for him. I poured every cell, every thought, into that frequency. Not fear. Not pain. Just love, wanting him to know I'm "going out" aware, unafraid, committing my soul mission to being around him and taking care of him and his from Beyond…

And then as the hours passed and morning came, as the sky outside my window shifted from pitch black to soft indigo, something in me shifted too.

I Knew I Wasn't Going To Die

Nothing had changed medically. But everything had changed energetically.

That's when I truly understood what I had been teaching others for years: that we can reset not just our minds… but our bodies, our energy fields, our fate. Love is a higher frequency than fear. And in that moment, I reprogrammed myself with it.

I didn't just survive that night. I emerged with something far greater, the deepest clarity I'd ever known.

This work, the work I now do with other women, isn't a theory or a trend. It's real. It's coded in our biology and unlocked by our willingness to go deeper, to feel more, and to stop lying to ourselves about who we are.

That was the night I remembered who I am. From that moment forward, I've been helping other women do the same.

The Pain That Programmed Me

They say you don't really know who you are until everything you thought you were is stripped away. But for me, that stripping began long before the hospital… My story doesn't begin at the brink of death. It begins at the edge of understanding, in a childhood shaped by mystery, medicine, and misfiring neurons, as a little girl whose brain didn't work the way everyone else's did.

From the moment I entered this world, I carried a body that didn't quite fit inside its own wiring. I was born after a complicated labor, and by age three, I had my first epileptic seizure. My parents, both doctors and highly respected in Romania, didn't quite know what to do with the child whose brain wouldn't cooperate, whose absences and seizures came without warning.

My father, afraid of the damage a grand mal seizure might cause, kept me on anti-epileptic medication for over 16 years.

I learned to live with aura, the eerie, almost psychedelic moment before a seizure hits, when the world blurs and shifts and your senses betray you. Most children feared it. I didn't run from it. I studied it. I mapped out how to walk to the chalkboard in school mid-seizure; I trained myself to navigate around desks and the blackboard without bumping into them during seizures; and I stopped mid-event in swimming competitions while in mid-seizure. I trained my brain not because I had a choice, but because I had a will. Even then, I knew I wasn't broken. I was different. And in some strange, spiritual way, gifted. I didn't know then that what I was doing was **neuro reprogramming**; I only knew I was determined not to be a victim of my own body.

I was the girl who couldn't tell her left from right, who couldn't read analog clocks, who didn't know if two musical tones were the same or different. Yet I became a **national champion swimmer at age 10.** Why? Because I figured out that the butterfly stroke, with its symmetrical movement, bypassed the coordination challenges my brain struggled with. So I mastered it. And it became my signature.

That kind of pattern, seeing what wasn't working and finding another way, followed me everywhere.

In my late 20s, I left Romania and moved to Canada, then eventually found myself in the U.S. Somewhere along the way, in my early thirties, I fell in love with Latin dance, salsa, bachata, rhythms I couldn't even hear properly. The irony? I was tone-deaf (Music is Math to me) and still neurologically "atypical." Still, I trained my brain on a treadmill, mimicking the motions and pacing until my body understood the music and found its rhythm, even if my ears didn't. I built new neural pathways, and eventually, **I danced.**

People began to say, *"You're such a natural."*

I smiled... If only they knew.

But even then, I didn't fully grasp the sacred mechanics of what I was doing, how I was reshaping not just my behavior, but my identity, my destiny, the very **architecture of my brain**. That clarity wouldn't come until years later… until the water.

I was 18, standing on the shore of the Black Sea, waves crashing around me like thunder. As a trained swimmer, confident and capable, I craved the sensation of moving against nature, so I dove in. But on my return to shore, just a yard from safety, I was caught in a riptide. The pull was violent and disorienting. I couldn't breathe. I couldn't tell which way was up. Pulled. Twisted. Lost. My lungs were burning, and I was out of breath. Somewhere deep inside, I accepted it, **I'm dying.**

But instead of panic, a deep peace came over me. I prayed. I remembered the white light I had felt in other moments of near-death. And then… I felt a hand. Not physical, but energetic. A **presence**, grabbing me by the back like a scarab and lifting me, guiding me, past the rocks, past the chaos, and into safety and calm.

I survived. Again.

That was the second soul reset. The first time Spirit intervened was my birth. From that moment on, I couldn't shake the feeling that I was here for something more, and that somehow, my brain, my body, and my traumas had all been preparing me for it.

This was my reminder. I wasn't just being protected. **I was being called.**

Over the next three decades, I became fascinated with psychology, neuroscience, spirituality, and trauma. I devoured books, attended trainings. I devoted myself to understanding trauma, consciousness, neuroscience, and energy medicine. I earned certifications. Built a practice and studied somatic therapies. In the years that followed, I developed my own methodologies. I combined neuro-somatic reprogramming, energy healing, EMDR, visualization, consciousness expansion, techniques most people don't understand unless they've lived what I lived.

I didn't just read the books, I lived the work. I began to integrate modalities like neuro-somatic reprogramming, EMDR, energy healing, and subconscious rewiring into my private sessions.

I've now spent over 27 years helping others, from neurodivergent children to high-achieving CEOs, understand, rewire, and reclaim their lives from trauma. I developed a results-driven process with consistent, measurable outcomes. But I still stayed behind the curtain.

You see, despite everything I knew and everything I helped others achieve, I was still hiding parts of myself. I wasn't yet living in full visibility. I wasn't yet speaking from the mountaintop. I was still dimming my light, telling myself that my role was to serve quietly.

Then Came 2022

By that time, I hadn't been sick in over 30 years. I rarely got colds. I was energetic, healthy, and vibrant. But then… my body collapsed. My lungs deflated. My iron levels hit zero. Blood clots formed. I had side effects from the COVID-19 vaccines taken months earlier and didn't even know it.

I told everyone I was fine for two months, but I couldn't breathe. I couldn't walk across a room without losing my breath. And still, I resisted going to the hospital. Until the day my brother called and heard me gasping for air.

He knew. He called our family in the U.S., yelled, begged, and urged them to get me to the hospital immediately. My mother, also a doctor, and my aunt drove from Virginia to Maryland, and my partner Doug stood there with tears in his eyes, pleading with me to go.

That day, I finally said yes.

And that night, as I lay in a hospital bed, lungs failing, unable to breathe, trying to text my brother *"I'm dying,"* **I had my third reset.**

Only this time, I wasn't alone. I had decades of healing behind me. Decades of sacred work ahead of me. And a soul-deep knowing that this was the moment I chose to live differently, not just for myself, but for the thousands of women waiting to remember their own power, too. I lived it all.

I've spoken seven languages and lived in different cultures. Navigated abusive systems. Discovered layers of my own identity that I once hid under labels like "neurodivergent," epilepsy, autism, adhd, or "high-functioning." I wasn't functioning. I was surviving. And eventually, **thriving.**

I always had an uncanny ability to see people's patterns, even as a child. I remember being in sixth grade and counseling a 20-something woman who tutored me in physics. I knew she was in a relationship with a married man, and I told her so, with calm wisdom well beyond my years. I didn't know how I knew. I just did. That's how Spirit speaks.

Eventually, all of it led me to my life's work. **Not a career. A calling**

Helping high-performing Gen X women, women like the one I had become, unmask the trauma they never had time to face. Women who showed up in boardrooms with polished nails and practiced smiles… while feeling dead inside.

They came to me exhausted. Scattered. Unfulfilled. They didn't even have the language for what was wrong, only a "knowing" that **this wasn't it.**

I showed them how to find "it." Not by giving them affirmations or to-do lists, but by guiding them inward. Deep into the nervous system. Into the trauma themes that had formed like layers of armor, trauma identities, protecting them, yes, but also imprisoning them out of alignment with the Higher Self, we dissolved those, one by one.

They became free. Some launched businesses. Others created new roles in their organizations that didn't exist before. Some saved their marriages. Others walked away from those who were never aligned. Many never needed therapy again.

Why? Because they didn't just get information. They got to **transformation.**

The same kind that brought me back from seizures. From drowning. From near-death. From shame. From silence.

And that's what led me to that moment in 2022, lying in a hospital bed at the Georgetown University Hospital in Washington DC, with five teams of doctors trying to figure out why I was dying.

I hadn't been sick in 30 years. But now, my body was shutting down. One lung collapsed. Clots. Zero iron. No oxygen. And yet… I knew something the doctors didn't. **I wasn't done.** Because I still had work to do.

The Moment I Knew I Couldn't Go Back

The morning after I thought I'd die, I opened my eyes and saw sunlight piercing through the blinds in my hospital room.

It wasn't just a new day. **It was a rebirth.**

I knew I wasn't going to die, not just because the doctors had stabilized me, but because something had shifted inside me. My love for my brother had kept me alive, but the bigger realization was this: **I was living below my own truth.**

I had spent years transforming others, watching women heal, rise, and thrive, but I was still hiding behind my own layers of resistance. I wasn't fully visible. I wasn't fully owning my story. **I hadn't let the world see All Of Me.**

And suddenly, I couldn't unsee that. The cost of staying hidden was far greater than the fear of being seen. If I had died that night, my work would have died with me. And that, I couldn't allow.

From Hidden Healer to Visible Force

After that night in the hospital, the night I almost died but didn't, I couldn't ignore the message any longer. I had spent decades healing others in private, unseen spaces. I had developed systems, honed my methods, and transformed lives. But I was still invisible to the world. Still shrinking in the name of safety.

The first step was simple, but not easy: **I said YES to visibility.**

I knew I had the tools. I'd spent over 27 years working with everyone from children and adults with autism to high-achieving executives. I'd built a results-driven program that blended science, spirituality, and energy medicine. My clients didn't just get temporary relief, they got measurable transformation. My outcome evaluations were consistently over 90%. But none of that mattered if I stayed silent. So I began to speak.

I started showing up, not just in session, but in conversations, on stages, and in writing. I revisited the techniques I had been teaching for years, not to change them, but to own them more fully. Internal Coherence and Consciousness Expansion became my flagship concept, a way to help women return to their truth and **recode who they are from the inside out.**

I stopped hiding my spiritual gifts. I let people see the woman who had danced through neurological limitations, who had healed childhood epilepsy, who had survived drowning and collapsed lungs, not as a victim, but as a living blueprint of what's possible.

I tested every method on myself, visualization, neurosomatic integration, EMDR, trauma reprogramming, archetypal embodiment, not because I read about them in a book, but because my life demanded it.

What I discovered through that process is something I've since seen reflected in the journeys of others who've faced similar life-or-death thresholds, people like Anita Moorjani, Dr. Joe Dispenza, and Dr. Eben Alexander, all of whom emerged from catastrophic health crises with **soul downloads, energetic upgrades,** and a mission to help others do the same.

I didn't read their stories and adopt their methods. I lived my own. But it's clear we're all tapping into the same higher intelligence, that undeniable truth that when the body breaks down, the **soul breaks through.**

From that space, I **codified my own transformational journey**, one that now guides other women, especially high-functioning, high-achieving

Gen X leaders, into a life that finally feels like theirs: free, embodied, and soul-aligned.

What moved me through the pain? The same thing that moves my clients every day.

The choice to stop surviving… and start remembering who we really are.

The Mess Behind the Mastery

People often look at me now, confident, clear, aligned, and assume I always had it together. They see my results, my waitlists, my transformational framework, and they think, *"Of course it worked for her."*

But let me be honest. **The road to get here was anything but straight.**

In fact, for a long time, I was my own worst detour.

After committing to live and lead visibly, I expected the shift to be immediate, powerful even. I knew my work was potent. I had over two decades of experience, multiple certifications, and a track record of outcomes most practitioners would envy. I had built a system that worked.

But translating that into a visible business? Into scalable impact? That was a whole different skill set.

I didn't know what I didn't know. And that ignorance cost me, in time, money, and missed opportunities.

I tried following generic advice from online coaches. I invested in programs that promised "six figures in six weeks," only to leave me feeling more scattered than ever. I wasted hours trying to master platforms and funnels that weren't built for a nuanced, deeply somatic, and trauma-informed practice like mine.

I tried to fit my magic into someone else's blueprint. And in doing so, I diluted the very essence of what made it powerful.

One of my biggest mistakes was thinking I had to "dumb it down," simplify the language, soften the message, strip away the spirituality and neuroscience, and serve it in a watered-down "life coach" package so that people wouldn't feel intimidated.

It didn't work, not for me, and certainly not for the women I was meant to serve.

Gen X executive women don't need fluff, they need depth. Surgical precision. They've already tried therapy, coaching, and coping mechanisms. They need someone who can see into the patterns and recode the Archetypes they carry in their Subconscious that they don't even know they're trapped in.

And for a time, I lost that clarity, **trying to be palatable instead of powerful.**

There were moments I questioned everything.

Maybe I wasn't meant to scale this work. Maybe I was supposed to stay invisible. Maybe being a "well-kept secret" was the safest way to serve.

The truth never lets you stay small for long.

Every client who texted me months after our work, saying, "I don't even recognize the woman I used to be," reminded me. Every woman who created a new life, new career, new identity from the inside out, reminded me. Every time I heard, *"You saved my marriage"* or *"You helped me find myself again,"* **Spirit whispered,** *"Keep going."*

So I did. I doubled down on alignment. I restructured my offers around the actual transformation, not what I thought would be easier to sell. I started teaching the real work, recoding the trauma themes **without talking about the trauma event at all**, because doing so can lead to further retraumatization. I embraced the metrics. 92-94% consistent outcomes. Measurable progress. Consciousness expansion backed by data.

I Stopped Trying To Go It Alone

I invested in support that honored the depth of my work, not just its surface-level marketing. I surrounded myself with women who saw me, the healer, the scientist, the soul-led visionary. I hired mentors who challenged me to show up fully, not shrink for the sake of being liked.

I still had stumbles. I still hit resistance. But now, every step felt guided. **Rooted. Aligned.**

Here's what no one tells you: the real transformation doesn't happen at the finish line. It happens in the weeds. When you're knee-deep in confusion and shame and self-doubt… and you choose to take one more step.

That's what qualifies me to guide other women. Not just the techniques. Not just the training.

But the fact that **I've been through the fire.**

I've wandered the weeds. And I've emerged, not perfect, but **powerful and clear.**

Which is exactly what I help other women become.

Dragon Strategies: How I Transformed and How You Can Too

As I walked through the fire of my own healing and growth, I didn't just change, **I transformed.**

I evolved from a behind-the-scenes practitioner to a highly intuitive leader who owns her voice and values. I deepened my frameworks. I refined my process. I stopped playing small, not just for myself, but because I realized how many women were waiting for someone to show them what true reinvention looked like.

Through this journey, I discovered that transformation isn't about becoming someone new. It's about remembering who you were before the trauma, before the roles, before the world told you who to be.

Here are the three core beliefs I now teach every woman I work with, My Dragon Strategies, and the real stories behind why they work.

1. **Reconnect to Your Higher Self**

You are not broken. You are under-downloaded.

One client, a high-level government leader, came to me fragmented after years of covert trauma, abuse, and systemic disembodiment. Through subconscious reprogramming and energy realignment, she was able to release old trauma imprints, stabilize her nervous system, and embody her true frequency, and conceived and birthed two children after multiple miscarriages. She now leads her life, and her family, as a mother, policymaker, from full alignment.

2. Rewrite the False Identities Created by Trauma

Healing doesn't just remove pain, it restores truth.

Another client, a high-performing executive, had spent years hiding behind perfectionism and people-pleasing, masking deep-rooted trauma. Together, we recoded her belief systems and built new internal architecture; she restructured her identity and reclaimed her voice. She now stands in an aligned relationship that honors her identity and has become a protector for others from abuse in her family.

3. Unleash Your Creativity to Manifest Your Next Chapter

Your soul expresses through creation, it's time to stop suppressing it.

A senior leader in a rigid organization came to the container muted and misaligned, and worked with me to reclaim her voice. As we reconnected her to her creative/ true essence, she stopped suppressing, and started shaping. She crafted a brand-new role within the company, one that didn't exist before, built entirely around her vision, skills, and values. Her next chapter wasn't found, it was created.

These are more than strategies. They are activations.

And every woman who dares to go through the fire… rises like a dragon.

Living the Dream and Inviting You In

Today, I wake up with joy in my chest and clarity in my bones. My life is no longer something I manage, it's something I fully embody.

I no longer apologize for how I think, how I feel, or how deeply I see into others. I move through life connected to my higher self, grounded in purpose, and guided by a mission that's been with me since childhood, to help others remember who they truly are.

I no longer shrink, filter, or hide. I dance, literally, on the treadmill at the gym while strangers smile and whisper, *"You must be a dancer."*

They don't know the years it took to get here. But I do. And now? I teach it.

I guide high-performing Gen X women, leaders, changemakers, visionaries, through the sacred process of reprogramming who they've been told to be, so they can finally live as who they've always been meant to be.

They come to me scattered and exhausted. They leave embodied, empowered, and wildly clear.

They become whole.

My vision is to awaken as many women as I can to their deepest truth, that healing is not a long, fragile road. It's a **powerful reclamation**, a remembrance. And when done properly, it's not only sustainable, it's magnetic.

If you're reading this and seeing any part of yourself in my story…

If you've checked all the boxes and still feel like something's missing…

If you're high-functioning but hollow…

If you've hidden your truth for so long that even you have forgotten what it feels like to be fully alive…

I want to remind you: It's not too late.

You're not too far gone.

And the life you dream of isn't just possible, it's waiting for you to **become her.**

Are you ready?

The next step in your story begins right now.

Marina Tudor

Marina was not born into coherence; she created it.

Diagnosed in childhood with petit mal epilepsy, autism, ADHD, spatial disorientation, tone deafness, and profound left-right confusion, her early life was shaped by sensory-motor fragmentation. Space, rhythm, sound, these were foreign languages to a body unsync'ed with symmetry. But from age three, she began retraining perception. She didn't just adapt, she recoded reality.

By age 10, Marina became Romania's national swimming champion in butterfly, transforming neurological chaos into disciplined form. She now speaks seven languages, guided by an autistic brain that hears "music as math." She holds dual BA and MA degrees, with a thesis on Emotional Reality, a healing modality she developed. She began her PhD work before transferring out to follow a deeper path of integration.

As a licensed psychotherapist (LCPC, NCC, CCTP, C-DBT, EMDR clinician), she's clocked over 20,000 client hours across the U.S. in trauma and crisis, autism, grief and loss, death and dying, and integrative medicine, backed by more than 54,000 hours of study. Clients report 92–94% transformational outcomes over the past decade. She specializes in neurodivergence, aging, crisis, suicidality, death, complementary and integrative restorative approaches, and the soul-body interface.

Marina has trained in over 100 seminars and crisis response programs, somatic work, and both top-down and bottom-up brain approaches. She's a Reiki Master in nine lineages and a practitioner of crystal and biofield therapies. Movement became medicine; salsa dancing is her long-term rewiring companion.

Twice rebirthed through profound soul-death experiences (at 18 and 46), Marina carries consciousness downloads that shaped her original therapeutic frameworks, rooted in post-traumatic genius, not pathology.

She is a living experiment in neuroplasticity and coherence re-patterning, and her life stands as quiet evidence that the human map, no matter how fractured, can be rewritten.

Marina Tudor
Mental Morphatrix MMTX
Rockville, Maryland
301-691-4015
Marina@MarinaTudor.com
www.MarinaTudor.com

Casey McDonald

Soul on Fire:
The Day I Chose Purpose Over a Paycheck

It was a painfully beautiful Southern California day in August 2018, the kind of day which made people want to play hooky, soak in the sun, and chase their dreams, but I wasn't chasing anything. I was stuck. Staring blankly through a dusty office window, I watched sunlight dance on car roofs and palm trees swaying in a freedom I didn't have. Inside, I sat motionless at my desk, trapped in a job which paid me too little and demanded too much.

The silence in the office was louder than usual. Phones didn't ring. Emails barely trickled in. My to-do list had long been completed. Yet I couldn't leave. I wasn't free to create or rest. I was just… there burning daylight, wasting energy, and questioning my entire existence.

I rested my chin in my hand, eyes scanning the parking lot as if escape might drive up and honk for me. My stomach sank with the weight of realization: I was trading my soul for a paycheck.

Years of effort, a business degree, certifications, a so-called "real job," had landed me here, bored, undervalued, disconnected from the vibrant life I'd imagined. I could feel my soul suffocating under fluorescent lights and unspoken expectations. The cruelest part? I knew I had more in me. I had already started building something of my own, a business which actually lit me up but instead of leaning in, I kept myself trapped in the illusion of security.

Then it hit me… **I don't belong here.**

It was my Soul on Fire moment, the day I chose purpose over a paycheck. Something had to change, and deep down, I knew I couldn't let another year of my life evaporate behind this window.

Long before that moment, I was a girl with big dreams, but no roadmap. The youngest of three girls, I grew up mostly like an only child. My middle sister lived with our grandmother, and my oldest sister was already out of the house. It was just my mom and me until she married my stepdad when I was eight. He was a Marine, which meant we lived a military life: structured, mobile, and financially tight.

We weren't poor, but we weren't well off. I watched my sister live a completely different life with access to travel, extracurriculars, and clothes I could only dream of. It wasn't jealousy, it was hunger. Hunger to experience more, do more, be more.

I wanted to live a life where I wasn't watching from the sidelines. I wanted to travel, make a meaningful impact, and have the kind of freedom I didn't see anyone around me living. Yet no one talked about how to get there. The unspoken rule was clear: get good grades, go to college, get a good job, and everything would fall into place.

So I followed the rules. I studied hard, became valedictorian, and earned a business degree. I believed I was doing what I was supposed to do, even though I had no idea what I actually wanted. I figured business was safe. After all, it "goes with everything," right?

Wrong…

No one told me a business degree doesn't teach you how to start a business. It teaches you how to work for someone else. It trains you to manage existing systems, becoming a dependable cog in someone else's machine.

After graduation, I tried to conquer the world, but the world wasn't interested. For years, I bounced from one temporary job to another, doing menial tasks for companies which saw me as replaceable. Eventually, I landed a "real job" at a small payroll company. It was stable, but stifling. I took the job out of necessity, not passion, telling myself every year, *"Maybe next year I'll leave. Maybe something will change."*

It wasn't just the long hours or low pay. I missed birthdays and holidays with family. I had to ask permission to live my life. I felt meant for more, but I was too scared to go after it. I played tug-of-war every day, between comfort and calling, fear and freedom.

From the outside, I looked okay. I had a steady job. I paid bills. Maybe this was just how life worked…but my soul knew better.

By summer 2017, something inside me shifted. I started asking harder questions: "Is this it? Is this the life I worked and fought so hard for?" I was tired. Physically tired, spiritually tired, tired of waiting for a life which never seemed to arrive.

That fall, I did something small, almost trivial: I booked something new for New Year's Eve, a little event to bring fun back into my life. That simple act cracked something open. It introduced me to new people, ideas, conversations, and possibilities. Hope sparked in a way I hadn't felt in years.

By April 2018, I started a new business. I didn't fully understand what I was doing, but I knew it was mine. I knew it had the potential to be something more than clocking in and out for someone else's dream.

For a while, I kept one foot in both worlds: the safety of my job and the promise of something better. That August day, staring out the window, I asked myself: "Why am I still here?" I had skills, fire, capability, but not yet the courage to walk away. Then the truth hit: I wasn't afraid of failing. I was afraid of never trying.

That realization was scarier than starting over. I didn't just want more money. I didn't just want more time. **I wanted purpose**. I wanted a life which actually meant something to the people I could help.

I realized I had been following a broken system. Education didn't equal opportunity. Following the rules left me stuck. I had seen countless brilliant, faith-driven women juggling family, business, and life while slowly burning out. They were doing all the "right" things, yet felt trapped.

I thought, *"What if I could change that? What if my pain became someone else's blueprint for freedom?"* That's when I realized: I wasn't just building a business, **I was building a legacy**.

Helping women break free from the hustle-and-grind mindset…

Helping them understand their finances so they could build real, lasting wealth…

Helping them reclaim their freedom, their joy, and their legacy…

From that moment, I knew: **I wasn't here to play small. I was here to light the way for others who were ready to rise.**

I had built a life which looked safe on paper but felt like a slow death in reality. Approval from people who weren't living my life. A paycheck which barely paid the bills. A routine leaving no room for dreams. Staying put wasn't playing it safe, it was self-sabotage.

Then came the quiet voice inside: ***"You were made for more."*** I didn't know exactly what that would look like yet, but I knew one thing: I couldn't keep betraying my purpose. Not one more day.

The first step was simple: say yes to something new. I accepted an invitation to a three-day event with a friend. There, I met people from all walks of life who had taken control of their time, their income, and their future. They were living their dreams, helping others, traveling, and building businesses. I thought: **This is it… This is what I've been looking for.**

I started learning everything I could about financial education, wealth strategies, and entrepreneurship. I found mentors. I asked questions. I failed. I got back up. I said yes again and again, to growth, to challenge, and to building something that mattered.

Within months, I launched my business while still working my full-time job. In February 2019, I walked out of my office. I didn't just fire my boss. I claimed my freedom.

The journey wasn't smooth. Wins came with setbacks. Leads ghosted me. Presentations failed. I burned through savings. I invested in programs which didn't deliver. I networked with people more interested in selling than supporting. I felt alone. I questioned everything, my competence, my calling, my choices.

The struggle shaped me. I realized the wins weren't just income, they were insights. I learned the difference between hustling for scraps and building a business which reflected my values. I learned going it alone isn't a badge of honor, it's a path to burnout.

Once I connected with aligned mentors and supportive communities, everything changed. My mindset shifted. My skills sharpened. I discovered wealth-building tools and strategies which surpassed traditional advice. I realized success could be ethical, sustainable, and value-aligned.

Walking through the fire didn't just build my business, it forged me. Every failure, hard conversation, and leap into the unknown became a stepping stone to a stronger self. I learned to lead by listening, seeing people, and helping them step into visions bigger than themselves.

I became a student of emotional intelligence, personal development, and high-integrity business. I attracted clients seeking clarity, confidence, and freedom. I began speaking on stages, coaching, and mentoring women trapped in the same "stuck" cycle I had once been in. I did it all without sacrificing my values or soul.

I learned to build differently, not around hustle or hype, but around legacy, faith, and truth. Now, I teach others to do the same.

Three truths I live by and teach every client:

1. **Formal education isn't the only path to success.** Alternative paths aligned with purpose often lead to greater impact.

2. **Traditional financial advice is often outdated.** Seek guidance from experts who practice what they preach.
3. **You were created for a purpose, and you already have what you need to fulfill it.** You don't need permission, just clarity, support, and courage.

Today, my life looks nothing like it used to, and everything is like the dream I once thought was impossible. I wake up with purpose, not panic. I work from anywhere, with people I love, doing work which changes lives. I spend more time with my family than I did in the tens year before I fired my boss. I've traveled, served, led, and grown in ways the girl at that desk staring out the window never imagined.

I'm not just living a dream. I'm living my legacy.

If any part of my journey feels familiar, know this… **You are not alone, and you don't have to figure it out alone.** There is a different way to build success, without burnout, brokenness, or betraying what matters most.

Your story doesn't end here. In fact, this may be the moment it finally begins. Take one step. The door is open.

Your legacy is waiting.

Casey McDonald

Casey works with established entrepreneurs who are ready to stop trading their peace, health, and relationships for revenue. She helps high-level leaders create true wealth across faith, family, fitness, fun, and finances so their success finally matches the life they want to live. As a Certified NLP Master and Approval Addiction Coach, Casey teaches the inner shifts most advisors never address, guiding her clients into freedom, fulfillment, and a God-given legacy which lasts.

Casey McDonald
Transcendent Wealth Architects
www.LinkedIn.com/in/CaseyWealthArchitect

Wealth Archetype Quiz: Unmask Your Wealth Superpower

Understanding your wealth archetype reveals the hidden beliefs and habits that drive your financial decisions. With this insight, you can break through barriers, make empowered choices, and chart a course toward lasting abundance. Take the first step to transform your financial story.

TranscendentGlobal.com/Wealth_Archetype

Melanie Love

Trauma. Truth. Transformation.

The Night Everything Changed

I can still feel the chill in the air that Sunday evening. Arizona winters don't bite the same way they do in other places, but the cold that crept into our home that night wasn't from the weather. It was the kind of cold that seeps into your bones, a warning from God, or maybe just my soul whispering, *"Pay attention. Something's not right."*

That morning had been strangely peaceful. We skipped church. Just the two of us at home, sipping coffee and savoring the rare quiet. After the chaos of the week before, I thought maybe—*maybe*—we were turning a corner. We laughed. We talked. We even snuggled under a blanket while the Arizona clouds gave us our version of a "cozy" day. Looking back, it feels like the calm before a bomb goes off. Because by nightfall, everything I thought I knew about love, safety, and myself would shatter.

Our son had just gone to bed. I remember the soft click of his bedroom door as it shut. That was the moment something in my husband snapped. I barely had time to turn around.

The next three hours blurred into one long, horrifying assault. It came in waves, three rounds, I call them now, like some twisted boxing match I never signed up for. There was yelling. Shoving. Fists. My body went numb from the adrenaline. I couldn't process what was happening, but somewhere deep inside, I knew: this is it… **This is the night I die.** I didn't. But I almost did.

And when I finally opened the front door, face swollen, body aching, soul cracked wide open, and saw our friend standing there, I said the only thing I could manage through swollen lips:

"Do you see my face?" He nodded, speechless. *"Good."* I turned, grabbed my son, and walked out not just of the house, but of the life I'd been silently surviving in for over a decade.

That night wasn't the end. It was the beginning.

Flashback to The Pain Origin

People always ask me the same question when they hear my story: *"How did someone like you end up in a relationship like that?"*

It's a fair question. I have a degree in social work. I worked with women escaping domestic violence. I *knew* the warning signs. I taught others how to set boundaries, build self-worth, and walk away. But what I knew in my head... didn't match what I allowed in my heart. And that's how these things happen, not all at once, but little by little. Like a leak in the foundation, you ignore it for years until the whole house crumbles.

I met him in my late twenties. I was recently divorced from the father of my oldest child and am not looking to date anyone. He was charismatic, charming, and so very sure of himself, the kind of man who could command a room and make you feel chosen just by looking at you. He was a salesman at a mattress store, where we met, and a man of God. And at the time, that was enough for me.

What I didn't see then—*or maybe what I chose not to see*—were the subtle cracks beneath the surface. The controlling comments are disguised as "concern." The emotional manipulation is framed as "spiritual leadership." The moments I was made to *feel small* so he could feel big. It didn't start with fists. It started with words. With isolation. With the constant drip of criticism that slowly eroded my confidence. My thoughts. My memory. My value. And I let it happen.

Because I believed love was supposed to hurt a little.

Because I believed God wanted me to be loyal.

Because I believed I could fix him if I just prayed harder, tried harder, stayed longer.

We had children. We had a church. We had a life that looked beautiful on the outside. But behind closed doors, there was chaos.

The truth is, the abuse was always there. It just didn't have bruises yet. He'd sabotage our finances without telling me. Then scold me for "not being better with money." He'd isolate me from friends and family, subtly at first, then more openly, until I couldn't remember the last time I had a safe space to share. He'd use Scripture as a weapon, twisting God's Word to justify his need for control. And because I was a woman of faith, I let him. I didn't question it… Not out loud.

I convinced myself it wasn't that bad. After all, he never hit me, not until that night. But abuse doesn't begin with broken bones. It begins with broken boundaries. And by the time I realized how deep I was, I couldn't see a way out. Not without shattering everything: my family, my ministry, my reputation, my entire life.

And yet, there were moments—*quiet moments*—where I felt the cracks in my own soul widening. Moments where I'd put the kids to bed, sit alone in the living room, and wonder, Is this what love is supposed to feel like? Where I'd feel a small voice inside whisper, **This isn't love. This is survival.**

I silenced it. I buried it under busyness. Under Bible verses. Under shame. And every time he'd snap, every time the mask would slip, I'd find a way to excuse it. He's tired. He's stressed. It's just a bad day. **I must have done something to set him off.**

It's wild how easily a woman can gaslight herself when the man she loves is the one holding the match.

Things escalated slowly but steadily, more yelling, more emotional outbursts, more nights spent hiding in the bedroom with the door locked, pretending not to cry loud enough for the kids to hear.

I knew the danger signs—*I'd taught the danger signs*—but I still clung to the belief that he could change. That I could change him.

Then came the 2018 Christmas break. We were fostering a little girl at the time. She had serious medical needs. She called me "Mom." Our biological son was eight, full of life and innocence. And the pressure in our house had reached a boiling point.

My husband's behavior had become erratic. I now know he was secretly drinking, hiding a deep addiction that made his mood swings even more terrifying. He'd come out of his study late at night, angry for no reason, picking fights over the smallest things. I stopped feeling safe. I stopped feeling seen. And one Thursday evening, he exploded at me in front of the kids.

That was new. That was a line he hadn't crossed before.

I tried to stand my ground, I raised my voice back, and both children burst into tears.

I spent the rest of the evening trying to soothe them, pretending everything was fine, while something inside me whispered: **This isn't fine. This isn't home. This isn't love.**

That night, I packed a trash bag with clothes and left. I didn't know where to go. So I drove to my office, a small converted home on an old military base, where I worked with women in crisis. The irony wasn't lost on me. There I was the helper, now hiding out in the same place I brought other women to for safety. I curled up on a couch meant for clients and cried myself to sleep.

Over the next few days, I stayed with a coworker. I emailed the deacons at our church, his church, asking for help. They didn't help me. Instead, they came and took our foster daughter. No one held him accountable. No one questioned his story. No one protected me. And when the social worker asked why I was so emotional, he told them I was "having a breakdown." And in that moment, **I felt it, the world shifting**.

If no one else was going to protect me… I had to do it myself.

Even if it costs me everything.

Even if I had to build a whole new life from the ashes of the old one.

Even if I had to do what I had been telling other women to do for years, walk away before it was too late.

That path wasn't easy. But it's the path that led me here, not just surviving… but healing. And eventually, helping other women do the same.

The Lightbulb Moment

I stood in the exam room, barely holding myself upright. My face was swollen. My ribs ached with every breath. The nurse whispered something and rushed out. Moments later, two police officers entered. And I remember thinking, *How did I get here?*

Just days earlier, I'd been folding laundry and planning our daughter's adoption. Now I was hiding from a man I once vowed to love, stripped of my dignity, trying to prove I wasn't losing my mind.

But when the officer gently asked, *"Do you feel safe going home?"* something in me snapped into focus. No. I didn't, and if I kept pretending, I never would.

In that moment, I realized, no one was coming to save me. Not the church. Not the system. Not even the people I thought would. **It had to be me.**

If I wanted to live—*really live*—I had to choose it. Right now.

What Moved Me Through the Pain

After the police report was filed and my husband was arrested, the silence in my life was deafening. The chaos had stopped, but now I had to sit with everything I'd been running from, the trauma, the shame, the guilt, the loss of the life I thought I had.

I didn't know where to begin. So I started with what I knew.

I went to church groups, thinking I'd find safety there. But even among other believers, my truth was "too much." I could see it in their eyes, that wide-eyed discomfort when I mentioned the abuse, the prison, the bruises. Even when I shared the PG-13 version of my story, it was met with silence or shallow comfort. I didn't need clichés. I needed someone to hear me. But no one did. So I kept searching.

Therapists. Counselors. Group leaders. I tried to squeeze my story into the boxes they offered, but it never fit. I didn't want to be told what I *should* feel. I wanted someone to acknowledge what I *actually* felt.

Eventually, I realized: **I had to create what I couldn't find.**

I leaned on my education, my bachelor's in social work, my master's in theological studies with a concentration in counseling, and my near-complete master's of divinity. But more importantly, I began listening—*really listening*—to women like me.

Not to fix them. Not to diagnose them. But to hear them.

That became the foundation of my Trauma Transformation program, not textbook healing, but soul restoration. Where women could reclaim their voice, rewrite their story, and **remember who they were before the world broke them.**

That's how I got here. And that's how I help others get there, too.

Journey Through the Weeds

There's this idea people have, especially those who've never lived through trauma, that once you leave, everything magically gets better. It doesn't.

When I left my husband that night, I wasn't walking into freedom. I was walking into the wilderness. The first few weeks were a fog. I was on autopilot, shuffling between court dates, police reports, social workers, trying to keep life "normal" for my son while my own nervous system was still in shock. My face healed faster than my spirit did. I told myself I'd be okay if I just got busy.

So I did what I'd always done: **I took care of others.**

I threw myself into ministry. Volunteering. Cleaning. Organizing. Helping. Fixing. Because if I could do it, I wouldn't have to feel. That worked, until it didn't.

Eventually, all that buried grief started leaking out in the quiet moments: late at night when the house was still, or during a worship song that hit too close to home. There were days I couldn't get out of bed. Days when I couldn't stop crying. Days when I questioned whether leaving had really been the right decision at all. **The loneliness was brutal.**

Yes, I had family. Yes, I had friends. But very few truly understood. And even fewer knew how to help.

I remember going to a church group, finally working up the courage to share a sliver of my story. I didn't even go into detail. I just mentioned that my husband was in prison.

The silence that followed was deafening.

By next week, everyone knew. The whispers. The side-eyes. The polite distancing. I wasn't just grieving a marriage. I was grieving the community. Identity. Safety. And that stung more than I expected.

Therapy wasn't much better, at least not at first. My first counselor was kind, but completely unequipped. She looked uncomfortable when I shared what happened. She asked textbook questions, checked boxes, and prescribed "coping strategies" that felt more like homework than healing. I walked out of sessions feeling more alone than I did going in.

That's when it hit me: **the system wasn't built for women like me. It was built to manage trauma, not transform it.** I needed more than a list of tools. I needed someone who could see me, not just as a victim, but as a woman trying to become whole again. But I didn't find her. So I became her.

And that process? It was anything but clean.

I made mistakes. So many. I stayed silent when I should've spoken up. I opened up to the wrong people and got burned. I trusted too quickly. I built walls too high. I overshared with people who weren't safe, then shut down around the ones who were.

I tried to pray it all away.

I tried to work my way out of pain.

I tried to shortcut healing by pretending I was already healed.

But every time I skipped a step, I found myself right back in the weeds, angry, exhausted, ashamed.

I spent money on programs that didn't speak to my soul. I read books that offered neat formulas for messy emotions. I tried to map my pain like a project plan, because that's what the world teaches us to do: fix it fast, package it pretty, move on. But trauma doesn't move on. It waits until you face it—*really face it*—and then it controls you.

It wasn't until I stopped trying to be "strong" that I actually became strong. Not the performative kind of strength, but the kind that's rooted in honesty. Surrender. Faith. That's when things slowly began to shift.

I found a church where I didn't have to hide. A pastor who wasn't scared of my story. Women who didn't flinch when I told the truth. And for the first time in a long time, I exhaled. I wasn't too much. I wasn't broken beyond repair. I was human, and that was enough.

Those years were painful. Expensive. Messy. But they were also sacred. Because in those weeds, I found the blueprint for real healing. Not the kind you Google. The kind you grow.

And now? That's exactly what I help other women do, without the years of trial and error.

Because healing is hard enough, doing it alone makes it harder.

Healing didn't turn me into someone new. It helped me return to who I truly was, the woman I had buried beneath years of fear, silence, and shame.

When the dust finally began to settle, I noticed something: I was laughing again, playing again. Smiling without second-guessing how it looked. My daughter once said, *"You used to be fun... but I'd never seen it before."* That's when I knew: **I hadn't just escaped something. I had reclaimed something.**

I started showing up differently, not just as a mother or a friend, but as a leader, a woman of faith, and a soul who knew how to hold space for other women the way I once longed for someone to do for me.

I went back to my roots: My bachelor's in social work. The nearly-completed master's in divinity, concentration in counseling. But this time, I blended the head knowledge with **soul wisdom**, the kind you only gain in the trenches.

I created the Trauma Transformation program, not from theory, but from experience. Every module, every workbook, every prayer, every prompt, it's something I wish I had during my darkest days.

I'm no longer asking for permission to be who I am. Now, I teach other women to do the same.

Here are three truths I share with every woman I work with:

- **Your pain does not define you, your choices do.** What happened to you is not who you are. You get to choose how the story ends.
- **You don't have to stay broken to prove you were hurt.** You are allowed to heal. You are allowed to rebuild. You are allowed to rise.
- **You are not meant to do this alone.** Even Jesus brought friends to the garden. Keep searching until you find someone who can really hear your story.

Dream Life and Invitation to Join In

Today, I wake up every morning with peace in my home and purpose in my heart. I'm no longer walking on eggshells. I'm dancing in freedom. My laughter is real. My voice is strong. My life—*though imperfect*—is fully mine.

My children see a mother who is present, playful, and unafraid to take up space. My clients see a mentor who's walked through the fire and came out refined, not ruined. And I see a woman I had lost for over 16 years, finally returned to me.

But what matters most is this: **I'm not just healed. I'm helping.**

My **Trauma Transformation program** was born out of the very ache that once left me hopeless. It's the program I searched for and couldn't find, the one that bridges spiritual truth with real-world healing. A safe place to be raw. A roadmap to become whole.

If you're reading this and parts of my story feel painfully familiar…

If you've been silently surviving…

If you've tried therapy, prayer, pretending, or pushing through…

If you're exhausted from being strong, and secretly wondering if anyone truly sees you…

Then please hear me: You are not too far gone. You are not too broken. You are not alone. You are simply standing at the edge of your own transformation. And just like I did, you get to choose what happens next.

The next chapter doesn't have to be written in isolation.

Let me walk with you. Let's write your healing story, together.

Melanie Love

Melanie Love is a Clinical Pastoral Counselor, Medical Social Worker, and Christian grief and trauma counselor dedicated to helping women rediscover their strength after seasons of deep hurt. With more than twenty years of experience walking beside individuals through some of life's most painful chapters, Melanie has become known for her gentle wisdom, nurturing presence, and unwavering belief that healing is possible for every story.

Her signature six-week program, Trauma Transformation, was born out of her own journey of surviving domestic abuse, emotional devastation, and the long road back to herself. When traditional therapy left her feeling unseen and unsupported between sessions, Melanie created the structured roadmap she wished she had—one that blends clinical insight, faith-centered encouragement, and practical tools for everyday life.

Melanie also founded Grief Compass, a series of resources rooted in her original Triad of Grief theory, which identifies the three forms of grief, Physical Loss, Emotional Loss, and Mental Loss, and provides compassionate guidance through each. Her work serves women healing from trauma, navigating divorce, grieving miscarriage or child loss, or learning to breathe again after years of carrying invisible pain.

When she is not writing or meeting with clients, Melanie can be found behind her camera capturing the quiet beauty of the Appalachian mountains or enjoying time with her children and grandchildren, the greatest joys of her life.

Melanie Love
Melanie L Counseling
USA
MelanieLCounseling.com

Week One and Chapter One Trauma Transformation

A glimpse into the guided journey that transforms trauma into strength.

https://Trauma-Transformations.com/Week-One

Samantha Potter

The Catalyst

Stopping Time:
A single moment collapses the illusion of normal life and forces everything to stillness.

It was supposed to be routine.

I'd missed my mammogram the year before, so when things opened back up for a bit in 2021, still in the shadow of the COVID pandemic, I scheduled it at the imaging lab, along with my "annual" physical with my doctor that I'd also missed. And like every other mammogram I'd ever had, they called me back for follow-up imaging. I have dense breast tissue, and I had actually told the tech when I left two weeks before that I'd wait for her call for the reimaging appointment. This was nothing unusual. I saw my doctor the day before I was due for the follow-up mammogram, and we'd actually joked about me needing at least 1.5 mammograms to make a full set.

I changed into the thin cotton gown and followed the tech into the mammogram room. She positioned me in front of the machine, her gloved hands cool and efficient. After the new images were taken of my right breast, she mentioned seeing spots of calcification on the scan before she led me back to the changing room.

"Just wait here until the Radiologist takes a look," she said. *"Don't get dressed yet, as he might want to reimage."*

A few minutes later, she returned. *"The Radiologist wants to do an ultrasound. Do you have time today?"*

"Yes," I said, and deep inside, something shifted.

A few minutes later, I followed another tech into the ultrasound room, clutching the gown closed around me. I settled onto the low padded table, the tech propped up my left side with rolled towels behind my shoulder and hip, with me facing slightly toward her to my right. She turned the monitor, allowing me to see as she began to run the wand across my right breast. And there it was, a bright, formless shape that stood out from the surrounding tissue.

I didn't need anyone to tell me it didn't belong.

My breath caught. A silent moan pulsed through my chest. I didn't panic. I didn't cry. But I knew. I knew.

When the Radiologist came in, he confirmed what I'd already seen. *"There are actually two masses,"* he said. *"The larger is eleven centimeters in diameter. The smaller, eight."*

The room faded. The hum of machines, the faint buzz of fluorescent lights, the feel of the gown around me; all of it disappeared. All that remained was a quiet, immovable truth: my life had just changed. Beneath it all, a question I couldn't yet answer whispered through me.

"If this was my wake-up call, what had I been sleeping through?" While I didn't know what lay ahead, I knew this wasn't the end. It was the beginning of something I had not yet named.

Jumping Timelines

A look back through the past that shaped the present. Where service, loss, and resilience begin to braid together.

Before that screen froze my world, I was doing what I'd done for the past 38 years, guiding others through complex legal processes.

For the past 25 years, I have been the Senior Paralegal specializing in estate planning and probate for a small transactional law firm. I loved my job, not because of the documents or the legal jargon, but because of the people. I guided families through the most difficult conversations, helping them navigate grief, legacy, and the process of letting go. I became part of their story. Some of them had been with me for decades. I'd helped their parents, then them, and now their children. They trusted me. And I held that trust close.

But the firm changed. The boss who mentored me had retired. The firm had been sold. The values I held dear were no longer reflected in the office around me. The heart that once defined our practice faded into billables and systems. But I stayed. I stayed for my clients, and because I told myself I should.

Then came the diagnosis.

The tumors were large and aggressive. The doctors chose five months of chemo first, hoping to stop the progression and maybe shrink the tumors. Then, after ten weeks spent regaining my strength and rebuilding my immune system, I underwent a double mastectomy, radical on the right, where I lost 23 lymph nodes. After twelve weeks of surgical recovery, I was on the last phase of my active cancer treatment: five weeks of daily radiation.

It was during that strange in-between space, after chemo but before surgery, that something unexpected began to stir.

I had discovered the world of death doulas.

While my body was being stripped down and rebuilt, I learned how to walk with others through their own thresholds. I began my doula studies quietly, between medical appointments and rest, and finished my third end-of-life doula certification just as the radiation burns healed. It felt like coming home.

I founded Rubicon's Edge a year after my diagnosis. At first, it was a side gig, woven around full-time work at the firm, planning to expand once retirement came. I added life coaching credentials when people began asking me if I could help them navigate other life challenges, moving into all life thresholds, grief, purpose, major life changes, and reinventions. I still held onto the familiar corporate job with the security of a regular paycheck, until

August 2024, when I was called into a meeting with the partners.

"We're being acquired," they said. *"The new firm's only keeping the paralegal with the most billable hours."*

Of course, I had fewer billables. Five months of chemo, major surgery, and months of radiation and recovery, not to mention another series of reconstructive surgeries in late 2023/early 2024. How could I not have fewer billable hours?

What stung most wasn't the rejection. It was the timing. It was only five months before I would have qualified for Social Security. After 28 years, would it have cost them so much to offer a small bridge? A bronze parachute for nearly three decades of loyalty? Apparently, yes.

They thanked me for 28 years and sent me on my way. Bitterness and rejection burned hot. Still, beneath it all was a quieter knowing. I wouldn't have stayed, no matter what they offered.

In that moment, I realized the choice was already made.

Turning Point In Motion

The quiet ignition of change begins; awareness starts moving faster than circumstance.

I didn't have a single "aha" with fireworks or flashing lights. It came quietly, like a whisper that grew louder over time.

During treatment, I kept working, often from home, and when energy permitted, in the office behind a plexiglass wall, masked, cautious, but still showing up. People told me they couldn't believe I was still functioning. Still serving. Still caring for others while my body was fighting for its own survival.

Somewhere in the middle of that chaos, I found a thread that would eventually lead me out of the haze. I stumbled upon a profile online, someone who identified as a death doula. I'd never heard that term before, but something in me said, *"This is the next step."*

I began my training in those quiet weeks between chemo and surgery, studying while my body was still weak. By the time the radiation burns healed, I had completed three certifications. What I learned went beyond legal preparation, it was about presence, compassion, and honoring the thresholds of life. I realized I'd been loyal to a version of my life that no longer existed. I couldn't keep living by old expectations and call it strength.

I didn't know exactly what was next, yet I knew I was already becoming someone new. It felt like coming home.

I kept following the nudges. Over the next couple of years, I added life coaching certifications, including Positive Psychology Life Coaching, Root Cause Coaching, Quantum Release, and NLP. I wasn't just learning how to support others. I was learning how to reconnect with myself.

I answered an inner call to delve into energy healing. A year-long training qualified me as an intuitive energy healer, able to use multiple modalities to shift my own and others' energetic field, bringing clarity and balance; releasing energetic blocks; plugging and healing leaks of energy, whether caused by interactions with others or by our own inattentiveness. And once that was done, I dove into another year of training to work energetically with groups, organizations, families, relationships, and systems.

Crossing The Current

Learning to move with pain instead of against it, transforming resistance into forward flow.

By the Autumn of 2022, I formed Rubicon's Edge as a side business, offering end-of-life support while still working full-time at the firm.

At first, accompanying my clients through their final threshold at the end of life felt like a natural extension of my years in estate planning. Holistic, compassionate, and deeply supportive of both my clients and their families. But it quickly became something more.

Then the second spark appeared. As I walked with clients through the end of life, I realized these tools were just as vital for anyone facing any other major transition: divorce, career shifts, disability or illness, an empty nest, retirement, identity shifts, or even the quiet ache of realizing, I don't know who I am anymore.

I added coaching credentials to expand my work beyond the dying, also to encompass the living who were standing at the edge of who they had been, and unsure about who they were becoming.

And then came the third spark. Energy healing. What I thought would support my doula clients became an even more powerful tool for helping people realign with themselves in every kind of transition.

These weren't just certifications. They were survival tools. First, for me, as they helped me heal, reorient and reclaim myself after cancer.

And now, they're tools I use to help others move through their own pain and come out with purpose.

Through The Tangle

The struggle of rebuilding and redefining in real time. Where clarity is earned, not found.

I thought that once I had the certifications, clarity, and calling, the clients would just come. By 2023, I had built what I thought was a solid foundation. I was a certified death doula (three times over). I had multiple coaching certifications, energy healing training, a name, a website, and a mission… I was ready.

But the truth? Nothing happened.

I tried to ease into this new world quietly, thinking I could grow the business slowly on the side while I still worked full-time at the firm. But when the layoff came, the gradual plan turned into an abrupt leap. Suddenly, this wasn't a side gig anymore. It had to work.

I was completely unprepared for how hard it would be to figure everything out alone. I spent countless hours tweaking my website, creating content, and trying to explain services that people didn't even know they needed. I offered everything I could think of, end-of-life planning, individual coaching, energy sessions, workshops, but instead of making things clear, I just made them more confusing.

People didn't get it. Heck, even I didn't fully know how to explain it. Some weeks, it felt like I was running on nothing but faith and stubbornness. I knew this work mattered. I knew it was needed. I'd seen it. I'd lived it.

I just couldn't seem to bridge the gap between passion and sustainability. And then came the doubts.

Maybe I started too late.

Maybe no one needs what I do.

Maybe this was just meant to be a passion project, not a livelihood.

Even then, deep down, the same part of me that woke up the day I saw that ultrasound screen—*the part that knew I couldn't go back*—refused to let me quit.

I asked myself the same question I often ask my clients, *"What is your soul really trying to do here?"* The answer came quietly, but clearly.

I began focusing on women, midlife professionals who have achieved much, yet quietly wonder when their lives stopped feeling like their own. They are accomplished, capable, and often exhausted by the version of themselves that once worked but no longer fits. They sense that something deeper is calling, though they can't yet name it.

From that realization, the Catalyst Intensive emerged. Not another coaching package, rather a precision process for profound transformation. It's the same framework that carried me through my own reconstruction, designed to help others dissolve what no longer serves and reclaim the self that's been waiting underneath.

It was never about adding more to their lives. It was about stripping away the noise, reconnecting to what was already true, and creating change that begins in the deepest layers; the ones no to-do list or motivational quote can touch. In those first sessions, I watched women's faces shift as something inside themselves reignited. Their energy changed. Their choices changed. And their lives began to follow.

Once I claimed that clarity, people began to respond. Not overnight. Not in floods. But steadily. Genuinely. With resonance.

Women began showing up who needed guidance, not convincing. They didn't want fluff. They wanted depth. They wanted someone who had been through the weeds and could walk with them, torch in hand.

Looking back now, I can see the messy middle was essential.

I didn't navigate this path only by classrooms and certifications. I forged it in the quiet, tangled moments when I questioned everything and chose to keep going anyway.

I tell my clients this now, with love and honesty:

"You can take the long road. You can try to figure it out alone, like I did. But you don't have to."

I'm here now, not just as a coach or doula, but as someone who has walked through fire and found the path forward.

In that heat, something unexpected happened: the fire stopped burning and started forging. What had once felt like destruction became refinement. The lessons hidden inside the struggle began to surface, not as pain, but power.

Tempering The Fire

Growth through friction: the refining process that shapes wisdom, skill, and grounded purpose.

Growth rarely feels graceful. It's more like being forged, heat, pressure, and the occasional roar from the part of you that refuses to die quietly.

In the months after I stopped trying to be everything for everyone, I learned that clarity isn't a single revelation. It's a practice. A muscle. And every time I trusted my inner knowing instead of the noise, that muscle grew stronger.

Building Rubicon's Edge into what it is now wasn't about polishing a brand; it was about letting my old identities burn away. The loyal employee, the careful planner, even the woman who thought her worth was tied to endurance, they all had to dissolve so something truer could emerge.

What I didn't know at the time was that I was building the framework that would become **The Catalyst Intensive**, a distillation of everything I'd learned about transformation: that healing requires both structure and surrender; that change doesn't stick unless the unconscious mind joins the conversation; and that true power isn't about force, but alignment.

Every Catalyst client begins where I once stood, aware that life must change but unsure how to begin. The Intensive meets them there, guiding them through three essential transformations in the span of only 2-3 weeks:

1. **Reclaiming Inner Authority:** We start by clearing the inherited noise; the expectations, beliefs, and stories that distort intuition. Without this, no lasting change is possible.
2. **Rewriting the Operating System:** Here, we dive into unconscious patterns using Root-Cause Coaching, Quantum Release, and Somatic Energy Healing to resolve what's been running the show beneath awareness.
3. **Resonant Activation:** The final phase shifts clients from survival to creation, recalibrating their values and beliefs to align with the life they actually want to live, not the one they've been taught to maintain.

The process isn't gentle, but it's liberating. And every person who completes it walks the path differently while becoming more awake, more attuned, more sovereign.

What I teach now isn't theory. It's lived practice, forged in the same fires that once threatened to consume me. That's what makes it real.

Living In Forward Time

Integration and embodiment. Standing in the present as both the result and the beginning of transformation. These days, I wake up without rushing.

I don't measure my value by how many hours I bill or how much I can carry for everyone else.

Now, my days are filled with purposeful conversations, not paperwork.

With soul-aligned clients, not endless deadlines.

With clarity and intention, not exhaustion.

I guide clients (mostly midlife professional women like I once was) through some of the most powerful transitions of their lives. Some are stepping into retirement. Some are rebuilding after loss. Some are simply waking up to the ache of realizing, I don't know who I am anymore.

And I meet them there. No judgment, only tools, space, and compassion.

The Catalyst Intensive was born from my own healing journey. It's not about bouncing back. It's about becoming who you truly are.

Here's what I now know:

- You don't need to start over.
- You don't need to have it all figured out.
- You just need to say yes to a new way of moving forward, one guided by your truth, not your obligations.

If any part of my story sounds familiar, if you've been feeling that quiet nudge that something needs to change, **I want you to know you're not broken. You are becoming. And you don't have to do it alone.**

The woman I was before cancer would have tried to muscle her way through. The woman I am now knows better.

This is your invitation, pause, breathe, and ask yourself:

What threshold am I standing at?

What would it mean to walk through it supported, seen, and guided?

If you're ready, I'm here. Torch in hand. Heart open.

Let's spark what's next, together.

Samantha Potter

Samantha Potter, the founder of Rubicon's Edge Consulting, guides professionals and leaders navigating pivotal transitions to awaken to a more purposeful, soul-aligned life. Blending neuroscience, energetic recalibration, and deep coaching to uncover and release unconscious emotions, she guides clients through the Catalyst Intensive, designed to dissolve old patterns, rewire the unconscious mind, identify values, and restore authentic alignment between purpose and action.

Known for her calm presence and rare ability to hold both complexity and clarity, Samantha brings grounded intelligence to the work of transformation. Her integrative background spans Positive Psychology, Root Cause Coaching, Quantum Release, NLP, Somatic Coaching, Hypnosis, and Energy Healing modalities, bridging Eastern, Western, and Shamanic principles to restore coherence between body, mind, and soul's purpose.

Through her signature Catalyst Intensive, Samantha helps midlife professionals dissolve inherited patterns, reclaim inner authority, release unconscious emotions, limiting decisions and beliefs, and rediscover and realign their values toward a more purposeful life.

Samantha's clients describe her as both strategist and seer, someone who understands the language of emotions and energy as fluently as she understands human behavior. Her work illuminates what lies beneath surface challenges, allowing individuals and organizations to release what no longer serves and create from a place of conscious resonance.

Known for her calm, grounded presence and her ability to hold both complexity and hope, she helps audiences rediscover self-trust, renew vitality, and become catalysts for change in their own lives and communities.

A U.S. Air Force veteran and lifelong volunteer, Samantha infuses her practice with a spirit of contribution and compassion. She has spent over forty years giving back to her community through literacy programs, disaster relief, education, and leadership in the National Novel Writing Month.

Samantha lives in the Inland Northwest with her husband and serves a global clientele virtually.

Samantha Potter
Rubicon's Edge Consulting
Spokane, Washington
509-425-3904
Samantha@RubiconsEdge.com
RubiconsEdge.com

Book a Clarity Call Today: RubiconsEdge.com/connect#clarity-call

Reclaiming What's Yours: Insight and Reflection to Help You Come Home to Yourself

If any part of my story sounds familiar, if you have been feeling that quiet nudge that something needs to change, I want you to know you are not broken. You are becoming. You do not have to navigate this threshold alone, and you do not have to figure it out by muscling your way through old expectations.

I want to offer you a space to return to yourself.

"Reclaiming What's Yours: Insight and Reflection to Help You Come Home to Yourself" is a free, seven-part email series designed to help you breathe and reconnect with what matters. Delivered over two weeks, these gentle reflections focus on reclaiming the essential parts of your identity that may have been lost amid the noise of transition: self-trust, values, forgiveness, boundaries, purpose, and resilience.

This is not a course intended to overwhelm you with tasks or push you to be "better". Instead, it is a structured inquiry to help you move through change with integrity. Along with the email series, you will receive the Reflection & Integration Journal, a digital workbook providing you with space to process your experience through grounding practices and body-based awareness.

https://birdsend.page/forms/12206/9Wv7RS8fki

Kathy Mayeda

Finding Balance in Chaos

Dusk was upon us as we were riding in a small regional park. My normally trusty grey Arabian, Beau, reacted to a "suspicious" rock, did a 180, and dumped me, somehow jamming the rude finger of my right hand. The shock of hitting the ground with my right hip shot through my body as I held on to the reins to prevent Beau from disappearing into the night.

I stood up dazed, took inventory of my body parts, found that my middle finger was shorter than the others (not normal!), and mounted Beau again to ride back to the boarding facility. Just one of many falls incurred while being an inexperienced rider on an inexperienced horse on the trail. "Green on green means black and blue." I was living that mantra.

I called the medical center, which informed me I should go to the Emergency Room, injecting fear of internal bleeding in my jammed finger into the conversation. I was X-rayed and was seen by the solemn ER doctor, who pronounced that I had a dislocated finger and a few bone chips. I thought to myself, *"No sxxx, Buckwheat."* He bandaged my finger into a splint, gave me a prescription for painkillers, and sent me home with instructions that I should get an appointment with a hand surgeon.

Two weeks later, I was sitting in the hand surgeon's office while he studied my X-rays and pronounced that I had a dislocated finger and bone chips. He told me I would never have a full range of motion in my middle finger again…

My whole body was racked from falling on my right hip, so I sought adjustments from my chiropractor. I told her about the prognosis that the hand surgeon had given me, and she immediately changed her demeanor from relaxed to angry and told me that I needed to call his office up and get immediate access to physical therapy, which I did immediately after her session. She started working on my finger, adjusting it and applying electrical stimulation, and told me to start icing it at home. I went to physical therapy over the following two months, along with chiropractic adjustments. It functions perfectly normally now, without any pain or stiffness, despite the prognosis from a hand surgeon at a prestigious medical facility. I started to distrust conventional medicine…

What started unraveling next was my journey into body awareness. I already had scoliosis… and maybe it's a chicken-and-egg thing that my scoliosis caused my imbalance for me to fall off in the first place. I have never been hospitalized in my life, but have had many minor injuries. I have a missing Anterior Cruciate Ligament and a partially ruptured and arthroscopically repaired medial cruciate ligament in my left knee from a previous ski injury. Fortunately, riding had stabilized my knee by working my quadriceps. I have had several automobile accidents, mostly being rear-ended, where my whole spinal column is racked.

Emotionally, I was a wreck during this time. I had a bad breakup with the breeder of my two horses, Beau and Beamer. I threw myself into my work, rising from a secretarial position to an electrical designer. I worked many long hours alone to fill the time. I had no work-life balance.

To exacerbate my work-life balance, I chose endurance riding, a time-demanding sport. My trusty steed, Beau, carried me through the twisty, turny, up and down trails through the mountain ranges in California, typically traveling 50 miles in a day during actual events, on top of many hours of conditioning each week. As a mid-pack rider, that meant four to six hours in the saddle plus a mandatory veterinary check with a maximum of 12 hours to complete the 50 miles during the competition. I was lucky to be at a boarding stable shared with several endurance stars who competed at the 100-mile-a-day level and learned the art of pacing and riding the trails at a pace far faster than the nose-to-tail dude ranch string could travel. Hours of conditioning required for the sport were my outlet, but it was also a lot of work, so it's questionable in the work-life balance equation.

The most crucial thing for me was having access to riding lessons from a world-class endurance rider at my boarding stable, along with her mentor, a senior-level Centered Riding instructor. Centered Riding is a system developed by Sally Swift, who had overcome physical limitations and created a teaching method to help riders ride balanced. Her work is derived from principles of Tai Chi and Feldenkrais, combining ancient and modern approaches to body awareness and movement.

I learned to ride softly, without muscle tension, and to apply soft cues to the horse without tension or resistance. I didn't bounce as much, and my balance on the bike improved, so I was able to flow with Beau as he navigated boulders and trees up and down the mountain trails. I also learned that when I thought I was riding straight, I wasn't. I had eyes on the ground to tell me when I collapsed to one side. I had to retrain my body to learn proper balance. My body had to accept a "new normal" that initially didn't feel like I was riding balanced.

My newfound body awareness inspired me to take Tai Chi/Qigong, Yoga, and Feldenkrais sessions to learn how to move my body properly through space. The only problem was that it confused me: yoga required muscle tension, while tai chi/gigong required muscle relaxation. Hence, taking the two concurrently as a beginner in both systems wasn't ideal. I eventually chose Qigong years later. Qigong taught me how to purge old energies and cultivate personal energy, to learn the ancient basis of martial arts, and to understand that they must learn to heal what they break.

While I was learning about my own body awareness, I had a steep learning curve in addressing Beau's physical imbalances. Beau had a lot of heart to be an endurance horse, but he had some balance issues that a seasoned competitive endurance rider would consider it less than ideal. He was taller than most Arabs in endurance competition, and his long legs wouldn't allow him to move with cat-like grace downhills like a shorter-legged Arab. At the beginning of our training, he was very difficult to saddle fit, causing his withers, the pointed part above his shoulders where the saddle rests, to lose muscle mass with poorly fitting saddles. He had a corneal ulcer scar from an injury that probably caused the accident in the park. He had what was diagnosed as an upward fixation of the patella on his left hind leg, which meant his leg would sometimes lock, and he would go momentarily lame. The cure for that was trotting uphill to strengthen his quadriceps, just as riding helped my quadriceps stabilize my left knee ski injury. His left hock would often wing out, and I had a talented farrier modify his shoe to minimize the winging until Beau was able to retrain his movement to track straight.

My riding partner had organized a horse care clinic with Diana Thompson, a talented horse trainer who had learned a huge bunch of tricks to rehab horses to full capacity. She evaluated Beau and noted that he had what is called "high-low heel syndrome," meaning his shoulders would be uneven, which was one of the issues surrounding our saddle fit woes. She gave me a fix: use shims to even out the saddle so I would sit balanced. Sitting imbalance increased his imbalance, and shifting my balance to be more correct allowed him to begin to move more balanced himself. She also taught a little bit of Bach Flower remedies, farrier science, and acupressure. This clinic proved to be monumental for me… Diana noted that I was naturally wired to do acupressure, which is the application of energy with fingertips on acupuncture points where licensed acupuncturists would actually use a needle.

I developed a hunger to learn about the biomechanics of the horse. I found Equinology, became an Equine Body Worker, taking as many classes as I could: saddle fit, farrier science, equine dental evaluation, and trigger point massage. I took these classes for pure enjoyment, not to be a professional, because I was still living the corporate life as an electrical designer. Along with these bodywork classes and watching many trot-outs during vet checks at endurance rides, I started to intuitively note where imbalances lie in the horse. I started to see energy that others could not, a slight hesitancy in one foot strike that would not be classified as a degree of lameness. Over time, it could lead to uneven wear.

I was able to manage Beau's imbalance issues, and we started to have real fun at endurance rides. I'll never forget the day that we were on our 3rd day of a multi–day ride in the desert near Death Valley. It was between Christmas and New Year's, so the mornings were crisp and the afternoons pleasant. It was extremely windy, and we were trotting by ourselves through the Joshua trees in perfect synchronization. We were in flow with each other and the Universe at the moment, and I didn't even care that my helmet visor was torn away and lost in the wind. I was in pure bliss. This is how it feels to be in total qi (energy) flow… timeless and boundless.

Back to "reality" in the corporate office, I looked through the Equinology course catalog for another diversion and found an Equine Craniosacral Therapy class. The prerequisite for the class was to take an Introduction to Craniosacral Therapy class from the Upledger Institute. I held a classmate's head and felt the therapeutic pulse for the first time, and I was so hooked… I immediately wanted to get certified in craniosacral therapy, and to do so, I needed to have some kind of healthcare license.

The easiest pathway to obtaining a license was to become a certified massage therapist. I quickly found out that most massage schools in the area were closing down. However, I found the local acupuncture school, Five Branches Institute, offered a certificate program in acupressure. Great! I flashed back to that clinic with Diana Thompson, where she said I had a natural gift for acupressure. Within the acupressure environment, I learned Traditional Chinese Medicine, Qigong (energy clearing and cultivation), and Tui Na (a massage technique). Everything fell into place… I cobbled together a mail-order class (this is pre-Zoom times) in Anatomy and Physiology, a Swedish massage class, an acupressure certificate, and all my Equinology coursework to become certified by the California Massage Therapy Council and get my business license to continue my craniosacral therapy courses with Upledger.

Meanwhile, my endurance career was winding down as Beau's hocks were fusing, and I had just obtained Drako. Drako was of show horse breeding, not sport horse like Beau and Beamer. He voted to be an arena horse after wearing me out trying to ride him in endurance training rides. He sent me into the world of natural horsemanship, where I learned to be subtle and patient.

Beamer, my first horse, who was a gift from my ex, returned to me after a breed lease, and I had many joyful trail rides with her.

Then my world as I knew it started to collapse. My beloved Beamer had a freak accident with a fence in the pasture and passed away. My parents' health was starting to fail, and my siblings and I had to navigate them into an assisted living facility. The financial crisis hit, and I was laid off from my last corporate job along with half of the company. I lived in the limbo of overseeing my parents' last days in the assisted living facility. I had opened an office for practice, but I had no energy to promote, so I eventually surrendered.

The worst was yet to come. Within the same week, my sister and brother-in-law uprooted and moved out of state, my cousin passed away with a freak horse kick to the head, and my father went into the hospital with pneumonia. I moved with my cat into a room in a stranger's condo because my house was being sold. I was house and horse sitting, so I was circling the Bay Area between my new home, the hospital, the house-sitting, and the boarding stable, the exact week when gas prices soared to $8/gallon. I got rear-ended at a stop sign in the middle of that torturous week. I had no feelings left when my dad left the world the following weekend.

The years between 2012 and 2020 were emotionally vacant. It provided a vacuum that I filled with personal growth and transformation. I continued taking horse bodywork courses and found another instructor who taught craniosacral therapy and osteopathic techniques for horses. My intuitive gifts started to grow during this time. Horses would give me the picture of the trauma that caused their malfunctions. Several of them involved severe biting abuse during training, causing malformed alignments in their teeth and jaws. I started taking occasional metaphysical classes because my brain needed to understand my intuition. The natural horsemanship clinics I took with Drako increased my capacity to understand how subtle energies could produce big changes in communication with another being. Beau passed away in my pasture during this time. My heart horse. He is still with me, as he sent Dado into my life to be a pasturemate to Drako.

I still didn't pursue healing as a career… I didn't want to market and expose myself to the public. I was hiding. I learned to quilt to pass the time. I was thinking that this is how the rest of my life was going to be. Little did I know…

I would visit my mother, grabbing sushi for a meal together and occasionally meeting my brother there, but other than that, I felt really alone, not knowing if I could ever be whole again. I would take her to many doctor appointments, be there for her many hospital stays. She passed away a week before the COVID shutdown in 2020.

All the pain that had been stuffed inside began to release during the shutdown. Along with the grief I felt with my mother's passing, I finally allowed myself to feel the loss of my father, who passed at a time when I had no nerve endings left. I was able to ride Dado in the park with a friend every week and get things off my chest. I took Zentangle, quilting, and metaphysical classes on Zoom. I was beginning to embrace the joys of retirement. However, the Universe had other plans for me…

After the shutdown, I started to take my massage tables to various healing shares just for fun. I would do craniosacral therapy among pranic healers, Reiki practitioners, and those who had no training. There were a couple of sessions that I was receiving my share, and I felt nauseated, paralyzed, and unable to understand what was going on. I asked my metaphysical teacher about it, but he had no answer, and I felt stymied and still vulnerable.

I happened to watch a Gaia episode with an energy healer, who taught via Zoom, and I thought she might have an answer. I signed up for Zoom trainings and eventually went to Montana for in-person training. Coming home, I was surprised by a couple of unsolicited requests for paid healings. One of them left the client feeling nauseated after the session. This wasn't the effect I desired.

At this point, a good friend pounded into me that I am spending all this money on education to gain skills I could market, and that I should be paid for an appropriate energy exchange for my work. So I embarked on the uncomfortable journey of an introvert, making myself visible so I can continue to manifest my true self as a healer.

A random email from a craniosacral therapy instructor caught my eye, and I signed up for her distance-healing course. I found that her method of asking the client to calibrate the amount of energy being applied was the answer. The techniques I learned previously poured energy into the client without this calibration; as a result, too much change was forced at once, causing nausea and discomfort. I learned to achieve a mutually grounded and connected state with the client. I started to accrue many sessions with people who were experiencing physical and/or emotional strain and became more grounded. I enable clients to get in touch with the unhealed trauma in a more neutral state to release trauma without totally reliving it. I was also healing myself in the process, and I started feeling whole again.

The state of being grounded and running my energy was also a key point of the qigong, martial arts, metaphysical practice, and Centered Riding instruction that I had been absorbing over the years. I also learned that breathing slowly and deliberately helps reset the nervous system and aids in grounding. My horse training clinics helped me not rush, engage in soft movements, and stay grounded to have the most effect. Being grounded has also brought many synchronicities that have tractor-beamed my Mission of Healing into creation.

Let me help you experience being grounded for your own healing and manifestations.

Kathy Mayeda

Kathy Mayeda was always obsessed with horses from a toddler on her rocking horse, begging for riding lessons in her pre-teen years, and imagining that a wooden structure being built on her dad's chrysanthemum nursery in Mountain View, California, was finally going to house the horse of her dreams. NOT. Kathy still had manifestation skills, but it was a double-edged sword. Horses came to her as a gift from her partner in her mid-life years, only to break up with him a year later. The horses were the vehicle that carried her from being alone with her grief and overworking as an electrical designer in a corporate cubicle to becoming an energy healer, now utilizing electrical currents in the subtle energy of the biofield. This path had opened up through wild synchronicity over the past two decades.

Finally accepting her mission, Kathy uses her virtual energy hands to help people let go of the life traumas that caused the physical and emotional pain. She soon realized that this wasn't enough to just release pain, so she developed the Triality Healing Journey to create scaffolding to rebuild their new lives with grounded purpose, stability, and connection to balanced Body-Mind-Spirit.

Kathy currently lives at the edge of Silicon Valley with her oversized Australian Shepherd and two very high-spirited Arabian horses.

Kathy Lynn Mayeda
Wind Horse Integrative Bodywork
United States
Kathy.Windhorse@gmail.com
Windhorsecst.com

Danielle Felicissimo

When Systems Fail, Genius Suffers

When the System Drew the Line

I still remember the room. The fluorescent lights buzzed softly overhead. The table was too wide, the chairs too stiff, and the air felt heavy with the kind of silence that tells you a decision has already been made.

The principal didn't look at my brother when she spoke. She looked at a folder. *"We've determined that this school environment is no longer a good fit for him."*

I was fourteen years old, sitting beside my mother, aware that I didn't quite belong in that room but unable to leave it. I didn't yet have the language for what was happening, but I could feel it in my body. This wasn't about helping him. This was about removing him.

My brother was brilliant. Curious. Restless in a way that made adults uncomfortable. He asked questions that didn't fit neatly into lesson plans. He finished assignments quickly and then disrupted the room because his mind had already moved on. He could take apart broken electronics and put them back together, but he couldn't sit still long enough to satisfy a classroom designed for quiet obedience.

His clinical label was ADHD, but that day, he was just labeled a problem. The solution they offered was not support, but containment. A placement meant to keep him compliant and out of the way, a room designed to manage behavior, not challenge intelligence.

I watched my mother fight to keep her voice steady as she asked questions. I watched educators shift in their seats, uncomfortable but unmoved. And I realized something terrifying. If we accepted what they were offering, this would become the story of his life. That was the moment something changed in me.

I didn't know yet what I would do with that realization. I didn't know how deeply it would shape my future. But I knew, with absolute clarity, that the system wasn't broken. It was working exactly as designed. And it was designed to leave people like my brother behind. **That was the first time I saw how easily genius could be mistaken for a problem.**

How I Came to See the Pattern Everywhere

Long before that meeting in the school office, I had already learned how to be the responsible one. Not because I wanted to be, but because someone had to be.

I wasn't just looking out for one sibling. I had two younger brothers, and in different ways, both of them needed someone to pay attention, keep track, and help things hold together. Each of them had their own personality, challenges, and strengths. But the common thread was that the system expected them to adapt first, and support came later, if at all.

Without realizing it, I was learning how systems worked. **And more importantly, how they failed.**

I was high-achieving, and school came easily to me. I understood the material quickly and finished the work long before most of my classmates. The problem was rarely comprehension. The problem was boredom.

My mind moved faster than the classroom pace. When lessons dragged, I tested boundaries in small ways—talking too much, losing focus, and pushing limits just enough to stay engaged. I learned how to control myself when it mattered, but I was rarely fully stimulated. Because I performed well academically, none of this raised concern. I was seen as someone who would be fine. That assumption followed me into adulthood.

I moved into teaching, training, and leadership roles where structure was built in, and expectations were clear. On the surface, it made sense. I was good at explaining things. I was good at helping people understand what was being asked of them. But even there, I started to notice something unsettling. Adults struggled in familiar ways.

Capable people froze when instructions were vague. Deadlines were missed not because of a lack of effort, but because of overload. I watched professionals apologize for mistakes they didn't fully understand how they had made. These weren't unmotivated people. They were exhausted.

Decision-making grew heavier over time. Follow-through suffered as mental energy was drained, managing confusion and self-doubt. I recognized the pattern everywhere I looked.

Eventually, the question stopped being whether people were capable and became why so many capable people were struggling in the same ways.

That question pulled me back into learning. I studied education, leadership, and executive functioning, determined to understand how people actually plan, decide, and execute in real life. What I discovered reframed everything.

The issue wasn't inadequate intelligence. It wasn't a lack of effort. It was the invisible load placed on people inside systems that assumed limitless capacity.

By the time I sat in that school office years later, I already knew what was at stake. That moment didn't create my purpose. It confirmed it.

When the Numbers Refused to Be Ignored

There wasn't one dramatic moment when everything changed. It was the data.

As I began looking more closely at research, patterns I had long sensed became impossible to ignore. Employment statistics show that adults whose brains process information differently face significant hurdles in the job market. In the United States, **only around 40 percent of neurodivergent adults are in full-time work**, while vast majorities face unemployment or underemployment, according to the National Library of Medicine.

Burnout statistics were just as alarming. Data from SHRM shows that **44 percent of professionals report experiencing burnout**, with chronic stress and anxiety now considered a routine part of working life rather than an exception. But the statistic that truly stopped me was about decision fatigue.

Research from the **University of Cambridge** found that about **60 percent of executives and founders experience impaired judgment after prolonged decision-making sessions**. This means that as leaders make decisions throughout the day, their ability to think clearly and weigh options objectively deteriorates. That was the turning point.

This wasn't a motivation problem.

It wasn't a talent problem.

It was a systems problem.

If nothing changed, the outcome would have been predictable. Burnout would continue to be normalized. Decision-making would erode under constant pressure. Capable people would second-guess themselves into paralysis, not because they lacked ability, but because the cognitive load never let up.

That was the moment I knew this work wasn't optional. It was necessary.

What I Did When I Knew Change Wasn't Optional

Once I understood the scope of the problem, I couldn't unknow it. The first step wasn't a business decision. It was an educational decision.

I went back to school, not to collect credentials, but to understand how people actually think, plan, and follow through. I studied education, leadership, and the mechanics of learning and behavior. I immersed myself in research on attention, cognitive load, and executive functioning, looking for answers that went beyond surface-level productivity advice.

What I wanted to understand was simple but critical: Why do capable people struggle to execute what they already know how to do?

From there, I started testing what I was learning in real life. I worked directly with students and young adults at the point where expectations suddenly increase and support often disappears. I watched how small changes in structure could radically alter outcomes. Clear priorities. Fewer decisions. External systems that reduce mental load rather than add to it.

The results were undeniable.

People didn't need more motivation. They needed fewer unnecessary decisions. They needed clarity instead of pressure. They needed systems that supported planning, follow-through, and recovery when things went off track.

I began refining my approach, combining mindset work with practical execution support. Not rigid rules, but frameworks that helped people decide what mattered, sequence their actions, and finish what they started without burning themselves out.

Over time, this work expanded beyond classrooms and training rooms. I started supporting leaders and business owners who were drowning in decisions, stuck in cycles of overthinking, and exhausted by the constant demand to perform.

Every step is built on the last. Study-informed practice. Practice refined the systems. And the systems became repeatable. That's how my work took shape, not as a theory, but as a method grounded in education, leadership, and real-world execution. I wasn't trying to fix people. I was learning how to build conditions where success was possible.

The Long Way Around

From the outside, it probably looked like things were working. I had clients. I had momentum. I had proof that my ideas weren't just theoretical. People were getting results when they worked with me, and that mattered. But what no one could see was the friction behind the scenes.

My early successes were real, but they were fragile. Every win felt hard-won, and every step forward came at a disproportionate cost. I could help others create clarity, but within my own business, I was constantly rethinking, revising, and second-guessing. I made progress in bursts.

There were weeks when I was unstoppable. Ideas flowed. Plans came together. Decisions felt obvious. And then, just as quickly, everything would stall. I would get stuck choosing between options that all felt equally important. I would delay launches because I wasn't convinced they were "ready." I would revisit decisions I had already made, convinced I must have missed something. I spent an exhausting amount of time trying to get it right.

I invested in programs that promised certainty. I followed strategies that worked beautifully for other people but collapsed under the weight of my real life. I built systems that looked impressive on paper but required more maintenance than they were worth. Every time something didn't stick, I assumed I just hadn't committed hard enough.

That belief cost me more than money. It cost me time, confidence, and energy.

There were moments when I wondered if I was contradicting my own work. I understood, intellectually, that execution breaks down when systems don't match how someone thinks. Yet there I was, forcing myself into frameworks that demanded constant decision-making, relentless focus, and perfect consistency.

I was tired, but I kept going.

Some failures were quiet. A program that never fully launched because I kept refining it. A collaboration that fell apart because expectations were unclear. Weeks spent rebuilding something that didn't need to exist in the first place.

Other failures were louder. Missed revenue goals. Overcommitted schedules. That familiar knot in my stomach when I realized I had once again tried to do too much, too fast, on my own.

The hardest part wasn't the setbacks themselves. It was the isolation.

When you're the one making every decision, holding every plan in your head, and carrying the responsibility for outcomes, the mental load becomes invisible but overwhelming. There was no external structure to catch me when my focus dipped. No built-in pause when decision fatigue sets in. No one to say, *"This is good enough. Move forward."*

I kept thinking that if I could figure out the right system, everything would stabilize.

What I didn't realize was that the missing piece wasn't another tool. It was support.

The shift began when I stopped treating independence as a requirement for success. I started building accountability systems, not as pressure, but as protection. I simplified my decisions instead of optimizing them. I created fewer priorities and committed to finishing them before chasing the next idea.

Progress became steadier. Not perfect. Not effortless. But sustainable.

I learned that leadership isn't about carrying everything alone. It's about knowing where structure is necessary and where flexibility is non-negotiable. It's about designing a way forward that can survive real life, not just ideal conditions.

Those early failures taught me something no quick win ever could. Doing it alone is expensive.

Not just financially, but cognitively and emotionally. And the cost compounds over time.

That lesson changed how I work, how I lead, and how I help others navigate their own journeys.

Learning to Lead Differently

The real transformation didn't happen all at once. It happened when **I started showing up.**

I became more intentional about how I made decisions. Instead of treating every choice as equally urgent, I learned how to distinguish between what truly mattered and what demanded attention. That shift alone reduced more stress than any productivity tool ever had.

I also learned how to pace myself. I stopped equating speed with success and started valuing completion, recovery, and consistency. Execution improved not because I pushed harder, but because I stopped fighting my own limits.

As a leader, I evolved, too. I learned that clarity is a form of care. Clear expectations, fewer priorities, and realistic timelines didn't lower standards; they raised them. When people knew what mattered most and why, follow-through became easier, and confidence grew naturally.

Perhaps most importantly, I learned to work with my mind rather than manage it by force. I developed skills in planning, sequencing, and finishing that didn't rely solely on willpower. I built rhythms that allowed for focus, rest, and recalibration, rather than constant pressure.

Out of that growth came three beliefs that continue to guide my work and my life:

- **If it doesn't light you up, it will burn you out.** Meaning fuels momentum. When the work connects to purpose, execution becomes sustainable instead of exhausting.
- **Systems should support how you think, not fight against it.** The right structure reduces decision load, supports follow-through, and makes consistency possible without burnout.
- **Small wins matter more than perfect plans.** Progress builds confidence. Confidence fuels action. And action, repeated consistently, changes everything.

These lessons reshaped how I define success. Not as constant output. Not as flawless execution, but as the ability to lead with clarity, adapt with intention, and build something that lasts.

Choosing a Different Way Forward

Today, my life looks very different from the one I was living when I first started asking these questions. Not because everything is easy, but because everything is intentional.

I no longer measure success by how much I can push through in a day. I measure it by clarity. By follow-through. Whether the way I work actually supports the way I live. I make fewer decisions, but better ones. I protect my energy so it can be spent on what truly matters. And I lead from a place of alignment rather than exhaustion.

My vision now is simple and expansive at the same time.

I believe people deserve systems that support how they think, not ones that force them to adapt constantly. I believe leadership should create clarity, not pressure. And I believe success should be sustainable, not something you survive on the way to something better.

I see this truth reflected back to me every time someone shares a familiar story. The endless to-do list. The constant second-guessing. The feeling of being capable yet stuck, driven yet depleted. The quiet fear that maybe it shouldn't be this hard, but not knowing how to change it.

If any part of my story feels familiar, that's not an accident. **It's an invitation.** An invitation to question the systems you're operating inside of. To notice where decision fatigue is draining your momentum. To consider what might change if clarity replaced urgency, and support replaced pressure. Because when the right support is in place, something powerful happens.

Your strength stops being spent on survival.

Your mind gets quieter.

Your follow-through gets steadier.

And what's been in you all along finally has room to rise.

That's what I think of as **genius unleashed**, not more hustle, not more pressure, but the moment your ability can finally meet your environment. You don't need to become someone else to move forward. You need a way of working that fits. **You're not broken... the system is**. And if you're ready to explore what that could look like, the path forward is closer than you think.

Danielle Felicissimo

Danielle Felicissimo is a speaker, author, and decision-and-execution coach who helps high-capacity women entrepreneurs build businesses that grow sustainably without burnout. She specializes in supporting women who think and process differently and need systems that work with their brains, not against them.

With a background spanning education, corporate training, and executive coaching, Danielle is known for her ability to recognize hidden patterns, simplify complex challenges, and design practical systems that support consistent follow-through.

Danielle's work is shaped by both professional expertise and lived experience. Early in life, she witnessed how traditional systems often fail intelligent, capable people who struggle not with ability, but with attention, structure, and rigid expectations. That awareness followed her into adulthood, where she observed the same patterns repeating in corporate environments and later among entrepreneurs who were driven, creative, and full of ideas, yet trapped in cycles of overwhelm, indecision, and unfinished execution.

With more than two decades of experience as a special educator, corporate trainer, and coach, Danielle helps women reduce decision fatigue, regain clarity, and create supportive structures that sustain action. Her approach blends mindset coaching, executive-function strategies, and business systems design, allowing clients to scale their work without sacrificing their health, families, or sense of self.

Danielle holds advanced degrees in education and leadership and is widely respected for her work with women who feel stretched beyond capacity by traditional business models that demand constant pushing and self-override. Her mission is grounded in a simple belief: there is nothing wrong with these women. What they need is a better way of working that aligns with how they think, decide, and lead.

When she is not coaching or teaching, Danielle enjoys iced lattes, long walks to clear a busy mind, and spending time with her family.

Danielle Felicissimo
Dynamo Genius
Yonkers, NY
Support@DynamoGenius.com
DynamoGenius.com

Decide & Prioritize™:
A Brain-Friendly Clarity and Decision GPT for Overwhelmed Entrepreneurs

Decide & Prioritize™ is a calm, brain-friendly GPT for entrepreneurs who feel mentally overloaded, stuck in indecision, or pulled in too many directions at once. If your mind feels busy but unfocused, capable but exhausted, this tool helps quiet the noise so clarity can return.

Inside this experience, you will:

- Unload mental clutter without needing to organize it.
- Reduce decision fatigue by separating what matters from what does not.
- Clarify the decisions that actually need attention.
- Choose 1–3 realistic priorities without pressure or guilt.

This is not a productivity tool. It does not push hustle, urgency, or optimization. Decide & Prioritize™ works by reducing cognitive load first, then helping you make grounded decisions and clear priorities in a way that respects how real brains work. Use it anytime decisions feel heavy, or focus feels hard to find.

https://DynamoGenius.com/Genius-Unleashed-Book

Jannette Anderson

Living a "YES" Life!

The smell of cigarette smoke and fried baloney still permeates my memory of that tiny basement kitchen. I was five, barefoot on the scuffed linoleum, clutching a dog-eared library copy of *Heidi*. I'd read it so many times I could recite whole passages, but I wanted my own copy; something that felt like mine in a life where very little was.

So I begged, bargained, pleaded, and wheedled. My world-class Aries-child persistence would later become one of my business and life superpowers.

Finally, my mother snapped!

Her face twisted, and anger, shame, and exhaustion collided. *"We can't afford it!"* she burst out.

It wasn't the "no" that scorched me. I heard *"we have no money"* so often that it was basically the soundtrack of my childhood. It was the look. That flicker of defeat I saw in her tired, sad eyes.

Something cracked open. Even at five, I knew I never wanted anyone, not my mother, not me, not anyone I loved, to live with that look in their eyes. I didn't have the words yet, but the seed was planted: I wanted people to live "Yes" lives. Not by magic. Not by pretending, but by deciding.

Fortunately, children are simple. Adults complicate things. "No money" was the problem, so "get money" became my obvious solution.

I launched my first "bidness" that very week, dragging toys and household odds and ends onto the front lawn, scribbling prices, and selling everything that wasn't nailed down. By day's end, I had $13.72, a fortune for a five-year-old, budding entrepreneur!

I expected applause. What I got was my furious mother realizing I had sold her new dress and household necessities. The spanking was swift. The humiliation of going door-to-door to buy items back was sharper.

By adult standards, my first venture was a disaster. But by soul standards, it was ignition.

I had tasted agency. I was able to solve problems with action. And I learned two valuable lessons:

1. **You can change your circumstances through business.**
2. **Don't go into business with your family. (Semi-kidding)**

That spark became a lifelong fire to create "Yes" lives, not just for me but for anyone who dared to want more!

Chaos to (Re)Creation

My mother married four times before I was eight. Every marriage meant a new house, a new set of rules, and too often, new violence. I stopped learning classmates' names because I knew we wouldn't stay long. Mom could be charming, magical even, but she was also a constantly brewing storm. Alcoholism, hypochondria, and what I later learned was borderline personality disorder, turned her into a human landmine.

Her last husband looked like Santa Claus and would drag her into his meditation room to beat her.

For two years, I'd lie in bed praying she'd be alive in the morning and that she wouldn't be knocked unconscious, because then he'd come after me. We escaped one morning when Mom begged me through blood-caked, cracked lips and a swollen-shut eye to give a note she'd scrawled to my teacher.

You don't bring friends into chaos like that. You learn self-sufficiency early. Most kids play house. I ran one.

My early years forged muscles I later relied on. Resilience, resourcefulness, fierce compassion, and a huge capacity for problem-solving. But they also left scars. I learned invisibility as a survival skill, and I came to equate value with endurance.

Healing took decades, but as Kahlil Gibran wisely says, *"Sorrow carves a deeper well for joy to fill!"*

The work I've done, and continue to do at sixty-five and beyond, is what lights me up. I am still stupidly in love with coaching and training that ensures my clients and audience members can release surviving to embrace thriving, now, and as long as they are on this side of the dirt!

Your experiences, from triumphant to tempestuous, from the trivial to the traumatic, have given you the wisdom and expertise that others can benefit from as well.

My "Heidi moment" wasn't about a book. It was about longing to matter, wanting a choice, and wanting a life not shaped by other people's limitations and issues. I didn't know it yet, but that tiny spark would become my ongoing "Why" in life.

The Long and Winding Road

As I grew, traveled, worked, healed, and invested in personal growth, that seed sharpened into an abiding purpose that underscores everything I do.

I want you to get that you matter and live like you do!

Purpose, I learned, isn't a title or a role. It's the intersection of two things:

"What we're healing from and what we long for,
for ourselves and others."

I longed to matter. To be chosen over chaos. To be seen. To be put on the damn list!

So naturally, I want people to feel chosen. To feel seen and heard. To live with a "Yes" in their bones instead of a lifetime of shrinking because of other people's "No." And to live into that practically and profitably by pursuing the path of their pleasure!

Yes, through hard experiences, including molestation, poverty, and growing up too fast, I built armor that hid my light. But I also learned how to hustle. To take my destiny into my own hands. To be brave. Not fearless; just willing to act despite the fear I lived with.

I worked part-time from age nine to help make ends meet. By fourteen, thanks to looking older, I was waitressing in a lounge and saving enough to take myself to Europe on a school trip. That trip lit the travel bug that fuels my digital-nomad lifestyle to this day.

Thankfully, in my early twenties, a series of transformational workshops cracked me open, letting the light in and out. I reclaimed parts of myself I thought were gone forever. The impact was so profound that I trained to facilitate transformational personal growth work myself, and that is the work that fills my cup and sets me apart from other business coaches.

For the first time, I wasn't just surviving my story… I was using it.

I devoured 375+ books on business, psychology, marketing, and personal growth. I invested tens of thousands in training. I built four different businesses, reinventing myself as needed. I've had the honor of teaching at universities, speaking internationally, leading teams, and helping businesses scale by 46% to 320% and beyond. I've coached thousands of entrepreneurs to grow their impact and income, and I'm just getting started!

I also did my time in the corporate trenches, in roles from a printing press operator to VP of a Fortune 500 company. But after a couple of years, the politics and bureaucratic B.S. would choke the joy out of me, hastening me back to entrepreneurship, my first and forever love.

There were many achievements, accolades, and adventures. But was it easy? Oh hell no.

I went bankrupt.

I battled depression.

I lost my brother to cancer, my mom to a stroke, and now I'm losing my sister to heart disease.

I restarted my business, from scratch, multiple times.

And like many who grew up proving our worth through hard work (emphasis unfortunately on the HARD), I did it mostly alone, **a mistake that cost me years of peace and progress.**

Yet the constant rebuilding and reinventing weren't failures… It was training… It was finding my path for that next phase… It was being true to myself!

Resilient reinvention taught me to rise. Again... And again... And yet again!

It honed what I now teach every Maturepreneur who crosses my path: ***"Being unstoppable is simply a choice we make every day."***

The 3 Keys to Success

After all the twists and turns, three touchstones have become my clarity compass, ones I want to share with you:

1. Purpose

Knowing my "Why" has kept me committed for decades. Purpose isn't what you do, it's who you are. Your "Why" (why you do what you do) is your anchor. When titles fade, roles change, and life shifts… purpose remains. It's the note only you can sing in life's choir, and trust me, the music isn't as sweet without your note!

I'm often called the **Why Whisperer** because I help people name and claim their purpose in ways that transform their lives and their businesses. When you finally see the thread that's always been there, everything clicks.

That's why I give back by offering a few complimentary **What's My Why?** sessions monthly (Paid sessions at $497 are available on my website).

Grab your spot today:

https://jannettescalendar.as.me/VIP-WhyClarityCall

Use the code: Gift to receive your valuable session for free.

2. Entrepreneurship

As you can tell, I'm unapologetically biased. I believe entrepreneurship is the most direct way to take charge of our future. It's also the best personal growth journey you'll ever take. Because entrepreneurship is not just a career path--it's a journey of reclamation.

To help you clarify your purpose and be more visible, download my free guide, **From Overlooked to Overbooked: Turn Wisdom Into Wealth Now!**: https://maturepreneur.world/wisdomtowealth

If you've ever felt invisible, this guide gives you tools to change that now!

3. Support

This lesson took me the longest to learn. Did you read the part about being a stubborn Aries!?!

Strength is not doing everything alone. Strength is choosing not to.

Every leap I've taken was because mentors, friends, and coaches believed in me. We all need support: practical, emotional, strategic. Success is a team sport, no matter how late in life we decide to play. You don't have to do this alone. In fact, you can't!

The Rise of the Maturepreneur: A New Yes!

In 2020, I was rudely dismissed at a networking event because of my age. Not my credibility. Not my contribution. My age.

Frankly, it pissed me off. I've been the subject of sizism and sexism in the past… but this was one ism too many! It lit a fire that still fuels my days.

If someone as visible as me, with my blue hair, polka-dot glasses, and 40 years of expertise, could be overlooked, what about the millions of brilliant, experienced, talented people 55+ who are dismissed every single day? No way, sister—not on my watch!

So I founded the **Maturepreneur World**. A mindset, a community, and a movement for those who are **#NotDoneByALongshot.** Did you know…

- Boomers and Gen X are the largest rising wave of entrepreneurs in history.
- We control nearly 80% of the world's wealth.
- Yet we're often overlooked, underestimated, and pushed toward an outdated vision of retirement that only 20% of us actually want, or can afford!

I don't know about you, but I'm not here to fade out quietly. We are here to rise into our final, and often most powerful, chapter.

Because at this age, something magical happens:

We care less about being impressive and more about being impactful.

We stop asking for permission and start giving ourselves approval.

We realize that a "Yes" life is a choice and finally, blessedly, we are ready to choose it!

Now It's Your Time

If my story teaches anything, it's this: **Your past may explain you, but it cannot contain you.**

You get to choose who you become from here.

And the world needs what you carry now more than ever. Your perspective, skills, grit, wisdom, compassion, clarity, and lived experience.

This chapter of life? It's not the wind-down. It's the rise-up.

Your "Yes" life isn't about saying yes to everything. Say yes to the things that matter to you now:

- Yes to your dreams.
- Yes to your purpose.
- Yes to your voice.
- Yes to making a difference.
- Yes to building something with the time you have left.
- Yes to being visible, financially viable, and valued.

If not now, when?

We are in our final chapter, which means it's the one people remember. And it's **the one we get to write.** Not based on others' expectations and "shoulds," but on our choices and desires.

So pitter-patter, let's-get-at-er! Because you, my as yet unmet friend, are **#NotDoneByALongshot**

If you are ready to clarify your next leap, book a complimentary **What's Next Clarity Call:** https://jannettescalendar.as.me/WhatsNext. We'll map your next chapter and make it real.

Because it's time! Time for you to live your YES life!

Jannette Anderson

Jannette is the bold, brilliant force behind Maturepreneur World, where 55+ isn't a finish line, it's the launchpad.

She's the business expansionist, the Why Whisperer, and a master at getting the four inches between your ears working so your business can work! Her transformational Clarity Compass, Create Purpose and Profit After 55 workshop, "What's Next?" expert coaching, and Next Chapter Launchpad program are designed to help you be visible, financially viable, and valued.

She shows Maturepreneurs how to rewrite what success looks like after 55 so they can step off the sidelines and take the helm of their own purpose-fueled, profitable ventures!

Why? Because she knows that age doesn't make you obsolete, it makes you unstoppable.

Her mission? To make "retirement" the new dirty word, and elevate the undervalued wisdom workforce into the global economic powerhouse it truly is.

#NotDoneByALongshot!

Jannette Anderson: The Maturepreneur
The Maturepreneur World
Calgary, Alberta
Canada
403-615-3838
Jannette@bodacity.ca
www.Maturepreneur.world

From Overlooked to Overbooked:
Turn Your Wisdom Into Wealth

The How to Go From Overlooked to Overbooked guide has actionable steps to clarify your purpose and help you create credibility and authority quickly. This is about more than business, it's about building your legacy and creating your lasting impact.

https://Maturepreneur.World/WisdomToWealth

bitly

ChewHoong Koh

Breaking the Rules:

From Not Enough to Aligned & Abundant

The Letter that Broke Me

I still remember the exact shade of the sky that morning. It was overcast but not raining, a muted gray that made the world feel suspended, as if it were holding its breath before delivering something irreversible. I was 17, standing still, staring at the envelope I had just pulled from the mailbox. The Ministry of Education seal pressed into the corner did not look official that day; it looked final.

My fingers trembled before I tore it open. A tightness had already formed in my stomach, the kind that arrives when your body senses danger long before your mind accepts it. I unfolded the paper slowly, forcing myself to breathe as my eyes scanned the page.

Each subject I had pinned my future on carried the same verdict: **Failed.**

The sounds of scooters passing down the street faded into a distant hum. Even the air felt heavier. I stood frozen, the paper trembling in my hands, aware that something far bigger than an exam had just happened. I had flunked my college entrance exams. The path I had been told to work toward, the respectable path, the secure path, had disappeared in a single sheet of paper.

I couldn’t even cry. Not yet.

Shame arrived first, thick, choking, immediate.

In my family, this was not simply disappointing. My parents were educators; achievement was not encouraged, it was expected. It was how worth was measured. I had watched students publicly scolded for poor performance. I had felt the sting of a ruler across my own hands for failing to sit quietly in a system that prized obedience over curiosity.

Now I held confirmation of what I had feared for years: I was not smart enough.

The Mask of Not Enough

Long before the letter arrived, before the failure, with my future slipping through my fingers, I had already learned to wear a mask, the mask of "not enough."

I grew up in a family of nine children in Malaysia, in a home where excellence was not optional. My father was a school principal. My mother was a teacher. Education was not simply a pathway; it was proof of discipline and character. Success was visible, ranked, and compared.

Many of my siblings seemed to do well within that framework. They brought home good grades and trophies. Teachers praised them. My parents beamed. I wanted that look of pride directed at me.

But **I… was different.**

In the classroom, the rules were clear: be quiet, memorize the material, reproduce it correctly. I was energetic, talkative, and curious. My mind jumped ahead, wandering into possibilities beyond the lesson. I asked questions, sometimes too many. My way of thinking did not appear impressive; it was labeled disruptive.

School became a battlefield. If I struggled, I was told I lacked effort. If I felt restless, I was told I lacked discipline. If I fell short, I was told I lacked intelligence. The conclusion was always the same: I was the problem.

I remember the sting of a wooden ruler striking my hands. I remember the sideways glances from classmates, the heat rising in my cheeks while I swallowed humiliation.

Worse yet, at home, there was no safe space to unravel. With my father, a principal himself, discipline and performance were cornerstones. If I had told him I was being reprimanded, the blame would have landed on me.

"You need to try harder."

"You need to be more like your siblings."

"You need to behave better."

By 17, my self-worth was hanging by a thread. The exam results did not create the belief. They confirmed it. See? **You're not smart.**

And the shame? It ran deeper than ever.

You see, in Malaysia, failing the college entrance exams meant you were rerouted. I was placed in a "special" school to repeat my senior year. Our uniforms were different. Everyone knew what that meant. We were the ones who had not made it.

After school, I would change out of my uniform before walking home. I did not want strangers to see the uniform and judge me. But of course, the judgment had already taken root inside me. I could not remove the internal uniform I wore. The uniform of "not enough."

So, I learned to adapt.

If I could not be the smartest, I would be the nicest. I became agreeable, helpful, and accommodating. I learned to read rooms quickly. I perfected people-pleasing because belonging felt safer than authenticity.

Then life disrupted the script. A partial scholarship to study in the United States arrived unexpectedly. I felt both disbelief and fear. Surely there had been a mistake. What if I failed in college? But something inside me, quieter and braver than my doubt, said yes.

In that new environment, something shifted. I flourished. Professors praised my insights. Classmates asked for my help. I didn't know what to do with the accolades; it felt foreign. I graduated Magna Cum Laude, a distinction I did not fully understand until others told me it was a big deal. My boyfriend joked that he owed his own academic success to dating me. At graduation, his mother thanked me effusively, *"My son, a Magna! Wow!"*

The same mind. The same girl.

The difference was not intelligence. It was context.

For the first time, I considered a radical possibility: what if I had never been deficient? What if I had simply been measured by the wrong system? The thought did not erase years of conditioning. But it planted a seed.

Years later, even after building a successful corporate and entrepreneurial career, the old whispers lingered. I called it comparison-itis, the relentless habit of comparing myself to others and coming up short. Praise felt uncomfortable and fragile. There was still a part of me that waited to be exposed as less capable than others believed.

I knew I had something to offer. After all, many clients would tell me, *"You're a sage. You're brilliant. You helped me solve something in such a short time that I've been stuck on for years."* And I would smile, while privately discounting it.

Why? Because the girl who got smacked with a ruler, who hid her uniform, who didn't get into a local college, hadn't been seen, heard, or healed.

That's what finally led me to my life's work.

Eventually, I realized something deeper: external success related to strategies, the "how tos," is only 20% of the equation. The 80%? It's what's happening inside. It's the beliefs we carry from childhood. The insidious, tiny traumas we normalize. The protective "unhealthy" survivable patterns we don't even know are running our lives.

When I began doing the inner work, examining those beliefs instead of outrunning them, my purpose crystallized. Helping other service-based entrepreneurs not just to build a business, but first build alignment. Alignment with their soul, their mission, and their energy. To help them shed the masks, the inherited shame, the old programming, and reclaim the "genius" version of themselves.

Because I know what it feels like to believe you're not enough. And I also know how empowered you become when you realize… **You always were enough.**

The AHA Moment

The turning point did not arrive with fireworks. It arrived in silence.

After a strategy call, a client, an influencer in her industry, said with conviction, *"You see things no one else sees. You helped me unlock something I've been stuck on for years. I'm so excited I can now achieve my crazy big goals."*

I thanked her, closed my laptop, and sat alone in the quiet of my office. The words lingered.

Why did others see me so clearly… when I still struggle to see myself? Why did I still hesitate to own the very brilliance I helped others uncover?

I had built a business helping entrepreneurs reclaim their voice, yet I was still carrying the identity of the girl who believed she was deficient. If I continued shrinking, deflecting, and minimizing myself, I would not only betray my growth but also limit my impact.

The AHA moment made one thing undeniable: The rules I had internalized no longer deserved my loyalty. Something had to change. **I had to change.**

Walking Myself Home

That realization did not free me overnight, but it clarified something essential: no amount of external achievement would silence the doubt that still echoed inside me. I had built competence. I had earned credibility. What I had not built was the ability to trust myself without seeking proof.

In the culture I grew up in, mental or emotional struggle was seen as weakness. You endured. You performed. You did not admit vulnerability. Choosing to examine my own wounds felt almost rebellious. I began acknowledging the subtle, harmful little "t" traumas I had dismissed for years. I saw the limiting beliefs that quietly capped my potential and the protective patterns that once kept me safe… over-preparing for meetings, over-delivering beyond scope, staying agreeable even when I disagreed… but were keeping me stiflingly confined.

I knew I could not positive-think my way out of this. What was required was sitting still long enough to notice what I had been outrunning, dismantling stories I didn't even know I was living by, confronting what I had been taught not to question. I worked with coaches who examined not just my strategy, but the identity beneath it. Somatic practices revealed how shame still lived in my body, tight shoulders before speaking, shallow breaths in high-stakes moments, and a clenched jaw whenever visibility felt risky. I faced the younger, confused, frightened version of me that still believed for too long that she wasn't enough.

The process was messy, uncomfortable, and humbling. Some breakthroughs came through tears; others through outbursts of anger. Yet it became the most liberating act of my life. It redefined what breaking the rules meant. It was not rebellion for its own sake. It was the decision to stop outsourcing authority. It was the refusal to keep proving before leading.

I was walking myself home.

Journey Through the Weeds

Once I acknowledged my own genius, I assumed everything else would fall into place. Spoiler alert: it didn't.

Instead, I entered one of the most humbling stages of my journey.

I knew I was called to help service-based entrepreneurs build fulfilling businesses. I saw a real transformation in my clients. Breakthroughs happened quickly and deeply. Clients would leave sessions lighter, clearer, and more certain of who they were and what they were capable of. But translating that impact into a sustainable, profitable business proved far more complex than I expected.

I invested significant money and energy following prescribed formulas that promised predictable success. Revenue trickled in. Visibility increased. However, inside, something felt strained, not flowing. I wasn't failing. I was almost succeeding. The "almost" can keep you trapped longer than failure, because it offers just enough proof to continue, even when something feels off.

I implemented funnels and launches that looked polished but felt unnatural in my voice. Every time I approached a new level of visibility or income, I delayed decisions, tweaked offers endlessly, and told myself I needed one more certification before going all in. Deep down, I knew: It was me. I was still carrying patterns of perfectionism, "getting ready to be ready," operating from the old belief that I wasn't quite enough. Sound familiar?

I had one foot on the gas and the other tapping the brake. The friction between the two was exhausting.

At one point, I considered returning to something "safe." Corporate life at least offered structure and predictability, a steady paycheck. Clear expectations. No personal brand to uphold. But something in me refused to give up. This was my calling. I just had to learn how to thrive without burning out or selling my soul.

So I did what I now help my clients do.

The turning point came when I stopped asking, *"What else should I implement?"* and began asking, *"Where am I out of alignment?"* That question demanded courage.

I got radically honest about where I was out of alignment. I wasn't here to build someone else's version of success. I was here to build a business aligned with my values, my gifts, and my energy.

I began dismantling, not recklessly, but intentionally. I rebuilt my programs from the inside out, not from scarcity or comparison, but from conviction. I reclaimed my genius, my intuitive ability to pinpoint what was really keeping someone stuck, my gift for bringing clarity to complex inner and outer blocks. My confidence steadied, not because I had more tactics, but because I was no longer betraying myself in the process.

I embodied what I now call the **Soul-Aligned Success Method™**. After that, clients began reaching out without persuasion or pressure, not because of a viral reel or flashy ad, but because they felt the congruence. They saw how I showed up authentically, no apologies necessary. One client told me she finally felt safe enough to stop faking it. *"I finally feel like I can just be me and know I'm f***ing brilliant."* That moment meant more than any revenue milestone.

I won't sugarcoat it: the journey through the weeds was longer and more expensive than it needed to be. I wasted time, money, and energy doubting myself and following paths that were never mine. But the lessons taught me something invaluable: sustainable growth does not come from copying someone else's architecture. It comes from trusting my internal compass and building with alignment. Momentum no longer felt forced. Success felt inevitable.

And that is why I am so committed to helping others shorten that journey, so their transformation is not temporary, but lasting.

Phoenix Rising

If you've ever met a woman who's walked through the fire and come out glowing, not burned, that's who I became. I don't say that with ego. I say it with earned wisdom.

Looking back at the 17-year-old girl holding that exam letter that felt like a verdict on her worth, I no longer see failure. I see conditioning. I feel compassion rather than embarrassment. The girl who once believed she was not enough was never broken.

Breaking the rules did not mean rejecting discipline or abandoning ambition. It meant refusing to measure myself by standards that were never designed for how I am wired. It meant recognizing that my sensitivity was not a weakness but a form of perceptiveness. That my curiosity was not a distraction, but a vision. That my instinct to question was not rebellion, but leadership.

The greatest shift was not external. It was internal.

I evolved from a hidden helper into a powerful guide. From a self-doubter into a divine-led catalyst. From playing small… into leading big.

I do not hand my clients a rigid blueprint. I help them access the wisdom that's already inside of them. Because abundance does not respond to imitation or hustle, it responds to alignment. And alignment requires courage, the courage to question societal rules, to dismantle internal ceilings, and to lead from conviction instead of fear.

If you're feeling stuck, misaligned, or exhausted by chasing someone else's formula for success, here are three empowering strategies that will change everything:

1. **Soul Alignment:** Know who you are at your core. Own your values, your voice, your genius. No apologies necessary.
2. **Mission Alignment:** Clarify your big why. Anchor your business in your soul purpose, so your impact and legacy become inevitable.
3. **Energetic Alignment:** Your energy introduces you before your words do. Clear the internal blocks, and your outer world will shift in response.

These aren't just strategies. They're sacred recalibrations for the person who's ready to rise.

The Aligned & Abundant Life

Today, my life and work feel different. Not because everything is effortless, but because it is congruent. I wake up each morning, very thankful, feeling what I used to think was impossible: fulfilled, genuinely joyful, and abundant in my business and life.

No constant hustle. No quiet panic asking, *"Am I enough?"*

And the best part? I don't have to pretend to be anyone else to succeed. I don't shrink. I don't hustle to prove my worth. I simply lead from the most authentically powerful version of myself, and it's magnetic.

I now work with soul-led service-based entrepreneurs who are done with spinning their wheels and ready to align with their true power. I help them build six-figure businesses without betraying who they are, no more formulas that feel forced, no more strategies that suffocate their spirit.

That's what I want for you, too.

Maybe you've felt the pull, that quiet voice whispering that there's more for you. Maybe you've followed all the advice, taken all the courses, yet you're still stuck in that cycle of doubt, delay, or depletion.

If so, I see you. I was you.

But here's the truth: You don't have to do this alone. In fact, you shouldn't.

Because the most successful entrepreneurs aren't the ones with the perfect marketing plan, they're the ones who are fully aligned with their mission, their energy, and their soul's truth.

So if you're ready to finally claim the business (and life) that reflects the real you, the bold, brilliant, purpose-driven you, then I invite you to take the next step.

You've already walked through the fire. **Now it's time to rise and thrive!**

ChewHoong Koh

ChewHoong Koh is a Soul-Aligned Business Mentor and the creator of the Six Figure Aligned & Abundant Program™, where she helps service-based entrepreneurs catapult their income while embodying their most authentically powerful selves.

Her journey began in Malaysia, where academic failure at 17 shattered her confidence and reinforced a painful belief that she was "not enough." Years later, after earning Magna Cum Laude honors in the United States and building a successful corporate and entrepreneurial career, she realized the truth: success is only 20% strategy and 80% inner alignment.

Today, ChewHoong specializes in helping heart-driven entrepreneurs break free from inherited beliefs, comparison, and burnout so they can build businesses rooted in soul purpose, energetic congruence, and sustainable profit.

Through her signature Soul-Aligned Success Method™, she guides clients to create High Ticket offers, implement aligned systems, and generate consistent six-figure income without betraying who they are.

Known for her intuitive insight and ability to quickly pinpoint what's truly keeping someone stuck, ChewHoong empowers her clients to shed old conditioning, reclaim their genius, and rise into aligned, abundant leadership.

She believes abundance does not respond to hustle or imitation. It responds to alignment.

ChewHoong Koh
Founder of the Soul-Aligned Success Method™
chk.misc@gmail.com
www.ThriveWithSuccess.com

Soul-Aligned Success Blueprint™

How to Reclaim Your Genius, Realign Your Business, and Attract Clients Without Hustling

If you're exhausted from forcing strategies that don't fit, this blueprint will show you exactly where you're out of alignment and how to fix it. Discover the three core alignments that unlock clarity, confidence, and consistent income without betraying who you are.

www.ThriveWithSuccess.com/Genius-Gift

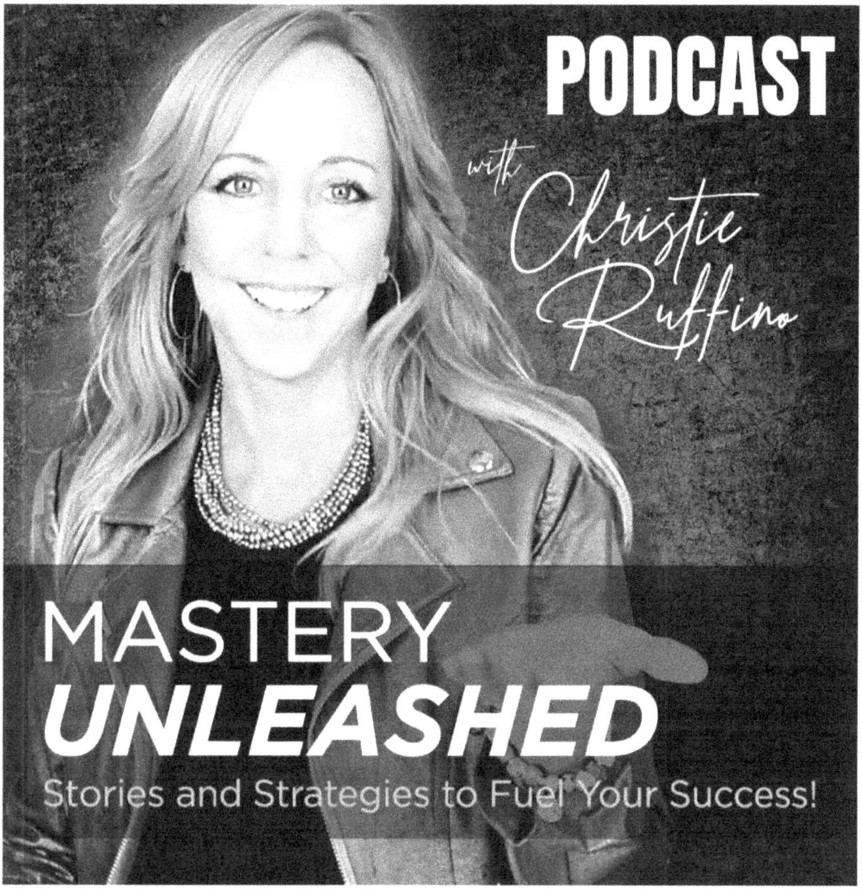

PODCAST

with Christie Ruffino

MASTERY
UNLEASHED

Stories and Strategies to Fuel Your Success!

Each episode features today's top influencers as they share empowering stories and ninja tips meant to become the

FUEL to IGNITE

a positive change in your life.

GET THIS FREE AI TOOL

Are You an Entrepreneur With a Story to Tell and Knowledge to Share?!

Get this easy, fast, and fun way to craft your signature brand story.

Story-Craft *AI* Super Prompts & Custom GPT

www.ingramcontent.com/pod-product-compliance
Lightning Source LLC
LaVergne TN
LVHW010057110826
845155LV00028B/382

* 9 7 8 1 9 3 9 7 9 4 3 7 6 *